SWEDEN

A Good Life for All

by Kari Olsson

Dillon Press, Inc.   Minneapolis, Minnesota 55415

Photographs are reproduced through the courtesy of the Minnesota Historical Society, the Swedish Information Service, the Swedish National Tourist Office in New York, and the Walker Art Center in Minneapolis. Cover photo by Dale Peterson.

Library of Congress Cataloging in Publication Data

Olsson, Kari.
  Sweden, a good life for all.

  (Discovering our heritage)
  Bibliography: p. 140
  Includes index.
  Summary: Presents Swedish geography, education, traditions, social customs, and sports, with a chapter on Swedes in America. Includes a list of Swedish consulates in the U.S. and Canada, and a glossary.
    1. Sweden—Description and travel—1981-   —Juvenile literature.   2. Sweden—Social life and customs—1945-   —Juvenile literature.   3. Swedish Americans—Juvenile literature.   [1. Sweden] I. Title.   II. Series.
DL619.5.47   1982   948.5   82-17683
ISBN 0-87518-231-3

Dillon Press, Inc., 500 South Third Street
Minneapolis, Minnesota 55415

Printed in the United States of America
2 3 4 5 6 7 8 9 10 91 90 89 88 87 86 85 84 83

Contents

Fast Facts About Sweden

Official Name: Konungariket Sverige (Kingdom of Sweden).

Capital: Stockholm.

Location: Northern Europe; part of the Scandinavian peninsula, Sweden is bordered on the west by Norway, on the east by the Gulf of Bothnia, and on the south by the Baltic Sea.

Area: 173,732 square miles (449,964 square kilometers); the greatest distance from north to south is 977 miles (1,572 kilometers) and from east to west 310 miles (499 kilometers); the mainland coast is 8,885 miles (14,300 kilometers) long.

Elevation: *Highest*—Mount Kebnekaise, 6,926 feet (2,111 meters) above sea level. *Lowest*—sea level along the coast.

Population: *Estimated 1982 Population*—8,369,000; *Distribution*—83 percent of the people live in or near cities; 17 percent live in rural areas; *Density*—49 persons per square mile (19 persons per square kilometer).

Form of Government: Constitutional monarchy; *Head of State*—king or queen; *Head of Government*— prime minister (appointed by the speaker of the parliament, or Riksdag).

Important Products: Livestock (cattle, hogs), milk and other dairy products, oats, sugar beets, wheat; cod, herring, mackerel, salmon; agricultural machinery, aircraft, automobiles, ball bearings, electrical equipment, explosives, household and office machinery, paper and cardboard, ships, steel, wood pulp.

Basic Unit of Money: Krona.

Major Languages: Swedish; English.

Major Religion: Christianity.

Flag: Yellow cross against a blue background.

National Anthem: "Du gamla, du fria" ("Thou Ancient, Thou Free-Born")

Major Holidays: Saint Lucia Day, December 13; Christmas, December 25; Flag Day, June 6; Midsummer Eve, the Friday between June 19 and 26.

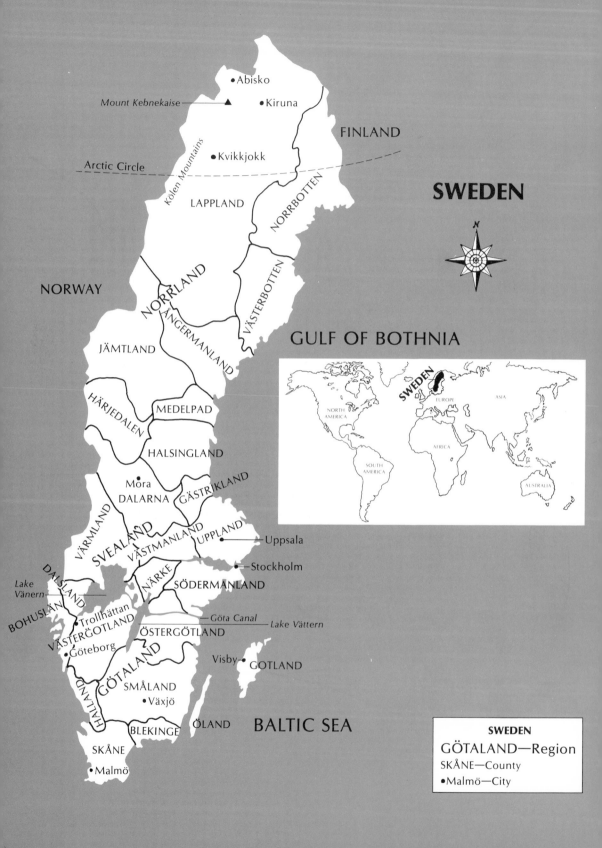

Abisko

Mount Kebnekaise ▲ Kiruna

FINLAND

Arctic Circle

Kvikkjokk

SWEDEN

Kölen Mountains

LAPPLAND

NORRBOTTEN

NORWAY

NORRLAND

VÄSTERBOTTEN

ÅNGERMANLAND

GULF OF BOTHNIA

JÄMTLAND

MEDELPAD

HÄRJEDALEN

HALSINGLAND

Mora

DALARNA

GÄSTRIKLAND

VÄRMLAND

SVEALAND

VÄSTMANLAND

UPPLAND

Uppsala

DALSLAND

Lake
Vänern

NÄRKE

Stockholm

SÖDERMANLAND

BOHUSLÄN

Trollhättan

Göta Canal

Lake Vättern

VÄSTERGÖTLAND

ÖSTERGÖTLAND

Göteborg

Visby

GOTLAND

HALLAND

GÖTALAND

SMÅLAND

Växjö

BLEKINGE

ÖLAND

BALTIC SEA

SKÅNE

Malmö

NORTH
AMERICA

SWEDEN

EUROPE

ASIA

AFRICA

SOUTH
AMERICA

AUSTRALIA

SWEDEN
GÖTALAND—Region
SKÅNE—County
•Malmö—City

1. A Land of Surprises

Sweden has many faces. It is a land of modern factories and of ancient forests. In places there are castles that are hundreds of years old. Not far away are gleaming new office buildings of glass, cement, and steel.

Sweden also has many different kinds of land and weather. In fact, on the very same day young people can be rowing on a lake in one village and skiing down a mountain in another part of the country. Likewise, people can be picking flowers in a lowland forest at the same time that others are warming themselves at a mountaintop fire.

Because your own country is so large, you may think of Sweden as a small country. This is not true. As European nations go, Sweden is quite large. In fact, only three countries in Europe—Russia, France, and Spain—are larger. If Sweden were one of the United States, it would rank ahead of California in terms of size.

Or think of it another way. Suppose you could lift Sweden up and lay it on the map of the United States and Canada. If the northern tip were placed on the border of the United States and Canada, Sweden would stretch down through North Dakota, South Dakota, Kansas, and midway into Oklahoma! As you can see, Sweden is not really a small country at all.

Perhaps you know that latitude measures how far north or south a country is from the equator. If you look at a world map, you will see that Sweden is in the same latitude as Upper Canada and Alaska. The southern tip of Sweden is farther north than Juneau, Alaska.

At first this would make you think that Sweden is a very cold land. But because of the Gulf Stream, it isn't. This warm ocean current from the Gulf of Mexico flows along America's southern coast, warming the land. Then it streams east across the Atlantic Ocean. Part of the Gulf Stream, called the North Atlantic Current, laps the coast of Norway and warms the winds that blow from the west. These winds keep Sweden's winters from being bitterly cold.

The weather does get cold enough to freeze all of Sweden's lakes and rivers, though. The cold even freezes the Baltic Sea, so that people can skate on it. Think of it—skating on the ocean!

The reason people can skate here is that the Baltic is not as salty as most seas. Salt is what keeps most oceans from freezing.

Winter is fun, but Swedes love summer. And those same winds that keep them warm in the winter keep them cool in the summer. Indeed, Swedes have the best of both seasons—snow and ice without too much cold, and sunshine without too much heat. This climate is all because of the winds and water.

Of course, we must not forget the part of Sweden that lies north of the Arctic Circle. That's a different story. Here the snow stays more than half the year, and it gets very cold. Worse, the days are short and dark. There is even a time when the sun does not shine at all. For weeks it is dark, dark, dark.

You can understand why if you think of the earth as a spinning tennis ball, and the sun as an enormous flashlight. If the ball is not tilted, it gets heat and light from the flashlight on all sides as it turns. But—here's the catch—if the ball is tilted, certain parts of it will receive no light or heat.

Like the tilted ball, the top of the earth is sometimes pointed somewhat toward the sun, and it receives light for a number of months. But at other times the top of the earth is tilted away from the sun. Then no light can reach the top, and it's dark there for many weeks. At the top of Sweden, there is no sunshine for two long months.

As you can guess, not many people want to live in northernmost Sweden. Those who do are mainly Lapps, a small, shy people who are not Swedes at all. You will hear more about them in another chapter.

But the Lapps don't brood about the dark time. They think of the time in the summer when the sun never sets for six whole weeks. Then it is just as bright at midnight as it is at noon. That is why Lapland is sometimes called The Land of the Midnight Sun. The long days of sunshine make a warm, bright summer.

The top part of Sweden is also called *Norrland*. In fact, everything in the north half of Sweden is lumped together with this name, which means north land. Norrland is the biggest part of Sweden, but few people live there.

The central area of Sweden is a lowland plain where most of the country's farming is done. It is not all fertile, though. Much of it is covered with lakes and forests. The whole area is called *Svealand*, which means land of the Swedes. It has been part of Sweden longer than other regions of the country.

South Sweden, called *Götaland*, is nearly all lowland, with lakes so long and close together that they almost stretch across the land. All of Sweden's large cities lie here. Here, too, there is much farming. The very tip of Sweden, called Skåne, is a rich breadbasket. This part of Sweden once belonged to Denmark, and the people still have Danish names and ways.

Everywhere in Sweden there is water. The coun-

Beautiful Tännforsen waterfall in Jämtland, Sweden, is 79 feet (24 meters) high and 198 feet (60 meters) wide.

try is crisscrossed by fast and foamy rivers that have many rapids and waterfalls. By putting dams on many of these rivers, the Swedes have been able to make electricity. But they miss the beauty of the waterfalls. And so one day a year, called Waterfall Day, the floodgates of the dams are opened. For that one day beautiful cascades like the one at Trollhättan can be seen again.

Sweden has many lakes, too—more than 96,000. That means a lake in every 1.8 miles (2.9 kilometers). Or a lake for every 87 people.

And would you believe that more land in Sweden touches the ocean than along all of the United States (excluding Alaska and Hawaii)? That's because of its wiggly coastline, which is full of bays and inlets. There are also thousands of islands called skerries. Some belong just to the birds. Others are vacation spots, dotted with cottages, where Swedes go to swim and sun. If you lived in Sweden, perhaps you would own an island.

Sweden has mountains, too. Much like the mountains in America's eastern states, they are beautiful in summer. Long ago, when summer came, young Swedish girls would drive their family's cattle into these mountains. The girls would then stay all summer, picking flowers, playing in the meadows, and making butter and cheese. When fall came, they would bring the cattle home.

During the winter the mountains are grim and forbidding. In some places there are glaciers, huge masses of ice and snow that have never melted. Because the climate is so cold, no trees will grow on the mountains above 1,600 feet (482 meters). But they are grand places for skiing. You can ski once around a mountain and be back at your own home.

Wind and water have carved these unusual looking stones out of rocks on the Swedish island of Gotland.

Parts of Sweden—more than half the country—are covered with forests. Miles and miles of dense, mysterious woods of pine, fir, and spruce stretch across the land. There are birch and aspen trees, too. Only northern-lake states like Minnesota and Wisconsin have the same kind of forests.

Where there are forests, you would expect to find wild animals. The fierce hungry wolves are gone. But there are still bears and lynx, along with small animals such as hedgehogs and badgers. If you see a huge animal with horns, don't call it a moose—it's an elk. You may see white-tailed deer and reindeer, too.

The lemming, a fat, furry, hamsterlike rodent, can also be found in Sweden. Every four years or so (nobody knows exactly why) lemmings seem to go crazy. They fight with each other, raise huge families, and rush off toward the sea. Yards, roads, and forests become a moving mass of brown furry creatures. Not many of the lemmings reach the ocean, though. Most of them die of starvation or are killed by other animals. Scientists think the lemmings are looking for new homes, but the lemmings do not tell.

You may think that a country like Sweden, with so many beautiful places, would be crowded with people. But it isn't. There are several large cities, but lots and lots of open space and wilderness.

Imagine taking a trip down Sweden's Göta

Canal. For three days you would float through forests and pastures. Perhaps you would spot foxes and rabbits. You might even be able to reach out and pat a cow! But you would see very few people.

Today there are not many farms in Sweden. Now nearly all Swedes live in cities, in modern apartments. Still, they love the country, and they often go there to spend weekends and holidays, especially in the summer. Every weekend, streams of cars leave the city, headed for the lakes and forests.

Swedish road signs would surprise you at first—the numbers would seem so large. That is because they show the distance from one place to another in kilometers. The Swedes have used metric measures like this for a hundred years. They say a distance is fifty kilometers, though Americans would call it thirty miles.

Until a few years ago, Swedes drove their cars on the left side of the road. But they decided that keeping to the right side was safer, and they changed their driving laws. In fact, they made the change overnight. One day everyone was allowed to drive on the left. The next day every car had to keep to the right. The Swedes don't mind changing things if they think a new idea is better.

Not everybody drives a car. In any city you see large numbers of people on bicycles—not just chil-

The Göta Canal is Sweden's chief inland waterway.

dren, but people of all ages, including doctors, judges, and shoppers. Old and young alike hop on their bikes and ride to work, stores, or schools.

Swedes have a good reason for using bicycles. Some places were built long before cars were even thought of, and many just don't have room for cars. Their narrow lanes, paved with bumpy cobblestones, are a rough ride even for a bike. Some streets are so narrow that a car can barely squeeze through. One street in Stockholm is only a yard wide, and some of it is taken up by steps. You can touch the buildings on both its sides with your hands spread apart! Nobody could drive a car there.

There is another reason you might not want to drive in Sweden—gasoline is expensive. In early 1982 a gallon cost about two times what it did in the United States. Besides, buses and trains will take you nearly everywhere. If you don't need to go far, you can walk. You'll see lots of Swedes doing just that.

If you are in Stockholm, there is still another way to get about. That is by water taxi. (Yes, I said water taxi.) This is a boat that takes you where you want to go. It's a good way to travel because Stockholm is a city of islands—fourteen of them. To get from one island to another, you can cross a bridge. But don't you think it might be more fun, and quicker, too, to go by boat?

No matter how you travel, you will meet interesting people. Many of them even look alike. Oh, not all of them, of course. Still, it is surprising how many of the Swedes are tall and blond, with blue eyes. Not, however, the king and queen—they both have dark hair.

Yes, Sweden has a king and queen. They don't have much to do with making laws, and they don't wear crowns, but they do live in a castle. The king is Carl Gustaf XVI, and his wife is Queen Silvia. The king's chief duty is to take part in ceremonies, such as the opening of the *Riksdag,* Sweden's parliament.

The real lawmaking is done by people who are elected to the Riksdag. At the head of the government is a prime minister. He chooses a cabinet to advise the elected officials. The people of Sweden do not need a king to rule them, but it is part of their old way of living to have one.

You have had a quick look at Sweden as it is now. It is a mixture of old and new. There are old churches standing near brand new skyscrapers. New mining takes place along with old reindeer herding. Travelers use old canals and new airports. Swedes are not afraid of new ways, but they are happy to keep the old ones.

King Carl Gustaf XVI and his wife Queen Silvia were married in 1976 and have three children.

2. The Middle Way

More than likely, you were born in North America. Probably your parents were, too, and maybe even your grandparents. But what about your family before that? Were they Scotch, German, African, Swedish, Chinese, or French?

Your friends live in North America, too. But most likely their family tree is not the same as yours. Our continent is made up of people with so many different backgrounds, we cannot imagine two North Americans who are exactly alike.

It is not that way in Sweden. Nearly everyone living in that country was born there, as were their parents and probably their grandparents. Very likely all of these people grew up not far from where they are living now. For four thousand years not much has happened to make them change their habits. There have been no invaders to bring new people or a different kind of life to Sweden.

Because there have been few outsiders, most Swedes have married other Swedes. We know this has made them alike in outward appearance. We should not be surprised that it has made their ways alike, too. As we visit their land, we will notice many

Like this young girl, many Swedes have blond hair and blue eyes.

ways that fit most Swedes.

The first thing we notice is the sameness of their last names. Many people of Swedish ancestry are named Anderson, Peterson, Olsson, or some other name ending in -son. That's because long ago there were no last names. A child was given a first name, with the father's last name added on to show whose family the child belonged to. A boy called Carl, whose father's name was Peter, would be known as Carl, Peter's son, or Carl Peterson. Only in the last hundred years has this way of naming children been changed. Today everyone is given both a first name and a family name, although the family name still often ends in -son.

Other Swedish family names were given to show the kind of place where people lived. *Dahl* meant that the family lived in a valley, *Berg* that their home was on a mountain. A family named *Strand* lived by the shore, *Gren* by a fork in the road, *Stad* in a city, and *Sten* by a rock. If you were to name your friends by the places they live, you would soon run out of words, wouldn't you? That is what happened in Sweden.

With so many family names being the same, it is easy to imagine the trouble you would have in trying to find a friend named Carl Peterson in the telephone book. There are a dozen pages of them. How can you find the right one?

The Swedes have tried to solve this problem by listing peoples' jobs along with their names in the telephone book. If your friend teaches school, you must look for teacher Carl Peterson. He will be listed after carpenter John Peterson but before travel agent Albert Peterson.

You can see from this that in Sweden it is very important to know others' titles. You also need to know them for another reason. When you are talking with someone you do not know well, you address the person by a title—Engineer Olsson, Dentist Johnson, or Plumber Anderson. And you must be very careful about saying *you*, because the Swedish language has two words for it. One you, *du,* is for people you know well, and love. The other you, *ni,* is for people you don't know at all, and don't care to know. Beware of using the wrong one! The only safe thing is to say, "Hello, Teacher Swensson. How is Teacher Swensson today?" When he thinks you know him well enough to call him Johan, or du, he will tell you.

Tak, meaning "Thank you," is another very important word that Swedes must remember to use. Guests at a meal should always say, *Tack for maten* ("Thank you for the food"). And if they meet their host the next day, they must say, "Thank you for yesterday." Being polite is so important in Sweden that you will probably never meet a rude Swede.

Swedes are friendly people, but they do not show their friendliness until they know you and are sure they like you. You could say that they are shy, or reserved.

They are also much more formal than many people would be. They want to shake hands with their friends each time they meet. That is their way of saying, "We are friends." If you do not offer your hand, they think you mean that you don't wish to be friends. Yet they will not force their friendship on you.

Deep down, Swedes are really thinking of others' feelings. They want people to know they appreciate favors. Yet they do not want to seem "pushy," and so they hold back. Someone has said that Swedish friendliness is like a bottle of catsup. At first nothing comes out. But once it starts, there is no limit.

Swedish children are taught very early that they must be *snäll*. This means being pleasant and polite, without squabbling or noise. There must be no dirt, disorder, noise, or pestering. No one should be grabby or selfish. Everyone must think of the rights of others.

Children are also taught that work is important. Even wealthy people keep busy. Swedes enjoy work and are very proud of what they can do.

This pride can be seen in a very old Swedish way

called *hemslöjd,* which means "made at home." For years people working at home have made many beautiful things. Among them are rya rugs, which are created by men as well as women. These rugs have a special knot that holds long strands of wool in heavy backing. The skillful blending of colors makes the designs works of art. Although the rugs are no longer used to keep floors warm, people hang them on their walls to decorate a room.

Homemade items are mainly useful articles because the Swedes like to be practical. Often the handcrafts are carved of wood, since Sweden has many forests. When a sailor was shipwrecked in Panama, he learned to make Panama hats. Soon the practical Swedes were making them in their homes.

Hard work has helped to make Sweden a land of plenty. Swedes have the most cars per person and the most telephones of any European nation. Every other family has a car. Nearly every home has television. The Swedes' standard of living (which refers to the things most people can expect to have) is one of the highest in the world.

Swedes have to pay for their good life with high taxes. They don't like paying these taxes, but they do like having a high standard of living for everyone. No one in Sweden is truly poor because the government helps those who are in need.

The government often aids people in paying for their housing. Most homes in Sweden are spotless and sparkling. Though not always new, they are often extremely beautiful. They are also the best furnished homes in all of Europe.

Once, the King of Spain paid a visit to Sweden. As his ship sailed into Stockholm harbor, he noticed a large and courtly-looking building. "That must be the Royal Palace," he said. "Fire a salute." Later the Spaniards found out that they had saluted the old people's home!

Cities are not only well-scrubbed and clean, but they are also neat and orderly. There is no trash on the streets—littering is something a Swede just doesn't do. The law says that waste paper must be collected.

Sweden is a wealthy country as well as a clean one. This wealth comes mostly from its exports because countries the world over are happy to buy its fine quality products. Swedish steel, long a term for the best and strongest steel, is used to make knives, forks, and spoons. It also goes into cars (Volvo and Saab), ships, ball bearings, and many other things that require expert workmanship.

Swedes are fussy about workmanship. They want a product to be as nearly perfect as possible. If it is Swedish, it must not be shoddy. You may have heard of Orrefors and Kosta Boda glasses, Hasselblad cameras, and other fine Swedish products.

One reason the Swedes have so many good things is that they are very careful with what they have. They have practiced forest conservation for a hundred years. For each tree that is cut, the logger must plant another, and every bit of the cut tree is used. The thrifty Swedes take care of their own things, too—the average family keeps its car fifteen years.

Orrefors glassware, made in Sweden, is well known throughout the world.

Although the Swedes do much to care for themselves, their government has tried to make a more comfortable life for everyone. Perhaps you know that it owns many mines and factories, and all the power plants. It also runs buses and trains, as well as the mails, radio, and television. Of course, many industries are owned by private companies, too. These businesses make everything from paper to aircraft engines.

Swedes also work in groups called cooperatives, or co-ops, businesses owned by the workers themselves. Co-ops make paper, flour, clothing, and light bulbs. In addition, nearly all of Sweden's milk, butter, and cheese come from co-ops, as does its meat. There are co-ops for travel, apartments, and pottery making. Swedes like to work together, so there are co-ops for almost anything.

The Swedes call their mixed economy the "middle way." They think it is halfway between having either private companies or the government own a country's major industries. In their view, everyone benefits from this system.

People in Sweden also believe that everyone benefits from obeying the law. Indeed, the Swedes are very law-abiding people. They need to be, because their laws have stiff penalties.

Besides the laws, there are rules for practically

every activity. On the Stockholm bus there are fourteen signs—everything from Don't Spit to Do Not
Disturb. Also, at a movie theater, people cannot sit
wherever they like. There is a seat number on their
ticket, and they must sit in that seat only.

The laws and rules are meant to help everyone
have a fair chance. There is even a person whose job it
is to complain. Called an *ombudsman,* this official
tries to see that nothing is done that would be unfair
to someone. If a bad law is passed, this person speaks
up.

Sometimes the ombudsman speaks up for the
rights of women. However, "women's lib" is no new
idea in Sweden. Even in the Middle Ages, when most
women were little better than slaves, a woman called
an abbess ruled over the monks in a Swedish monas-
tery. And Swedish women have been able to vote
since 1914. As for jobs, all lines of work are open to
them. They can be doctors, engineers, politicians,
dentists, or ministers. In fact, the next ruler will be a
woman—Princess Victoria.

When a woman with a family goes to work, she
can take her children to a public day-care center. If
she loses her job, she can receive money from either a
trade union or the government. And both women and
men can leave their jobs for a time, with pay, to care
for their children.

In spite of a life so free from trouble, visitors often remark that Swedes seem to be a sad and gloomy people. This may be partly because they have such long, dark winters and such short summers. Summer lasts only from June to August, and the Swedes can hardly wait for it. Once it arrives, they use every moment of it, swimming, boating, hiking, and sunbathing. Skimpy as most bathing suits are, some Swedes think they keep out too much sun. As a result, there are special areas where people may swim with no bathing suits at all.

Most Swedes love nature and all outdoors. You need not go far from the city to find yourself in a forest. You will also see flowers growing everywhere. Cottages are covered with climbing roses of a brilliant red color that is found nowhere else in the world. Fresh flowers are seen in homes every day, not just on special occasions. It is not surprising that the person who first learned to classify plants was the Swedish botanist Linnaeus.

Although most Swedes like to be outdoors, you shouldn't imagine that they don't have any differences. Just as a Texan does not speak or dress like a Vermonter, people in different parts of Sweden have their own special ways.

At one time each area had its own customs and costumes. You could tell if people came from Värmland or Blekinge by the way they dressed. Most men wore knee breeches and vests. Women usually had full skirts, with bodices, caps, and aprons. Differences in color or stripes told where the owner lived. Nowadays you would not often see these costumes. They are worn only for festivals or tourist events, where they help to show the color and charm of old Swedish customs. In their everyday life, Swedes dress much the same as people elsewhere.

Many traces of old Sweden can still be found, though. There are people in Visby called pure Gothics who speak a kind of Swedish not heard anywhere else for centuries. Dalarna is noted for its sturdy peasants and folk dancing. Skåne people (called Skonings) are almost like Danes in speech and manner.

The Lapps who live in the northern part of the country are an entirely separate people from the Swedes. Shy and gentle, they have long been reindeer herders. Though many of them have given up their old ways, some still follow ancient customs in the land of their ancestors. Even today you can see their bright costumes. Men wear a brightly-trimmed blue tunic, and the Cap of the Four Winds. This cap has a wide band of many colors, a top shaped into four floppy points, and many fluttering streamers. The Lapps also have their own language.

Now you can see why Swedes are Swedes, and

(Above) *People in Värmland once dressed in colorful peasant costumes.* (Right) *Men and boys in Lapland still wear brightly-colored tunics and the Cap of the Four Winds.*

not like Germans or Chinese. Their life-style has given them a certain way of looking at things, as well as their own special customs. Because of this life-style, a Swede named Carl or Kristin thinks and acts differently than a North American named Charles or Christine. We would not say that the Swede's ideas and customs are better or worse than our own. We only know that, in Sweden, we can expect to find Swedish ways.

3. Heroes Live On

Sweden's history is full of stories about kings and heroes. The oldest stories come from sagas, tales concerning brave and fearless deeds that were handed down from age to age by singers and storytellers.

Scientists have sought out the story of the past, too. Digging in forgotten places, they have found old bones, coins, and other remains which show that people lived in Sweden as early as twelve thousand years ago. Long before the Lapps, these vanished people were reindeer herders.

After these herders came people who raised cows and goats. Their houses were built on platforms, and they ate grain, cherries, and tiny apples. A skeleton of one of these people that is four thousand years old can be seen at Visby. It shows that they were very small people.

An early people called the *Svear* gave Sweden its name. Later the Goths moved into what is now southern Sweden. This area is still called *Götaland,* Gothland.

Traders from far lands came to buy furs from these Swedes. After returning home, they told their own people what they had seen. Old Roman writings say that the Swedes were very powerful men, skilled with boats and weapons. The ancient Egyptians put Sweden on their world map, calling it Scandia and showing it as an island. It was a strange place, the Egyptians said. For half the year, the sun rose as soon as it set, and for the other half, it was night all the time.

The old Swedes sacrificed human beings to make the gods happy. King Aun even killed his own nine sons so that Odin would grant him long life. The kings claimed to be children of the gods.

A seafaring people, the Swedes saw the riches of other lands in their travels. Some of them joined bands of raiders called *Vikings* that were beginning to swoop down on Russia, Ireland, Scotland, England, France, and Germany. Swords in hand, they stole people and goods, burning and killing what they did not take. The terrified people of other seacoasts prayed, "God save us from the cruel Vikings."

The name Viking comes from the old word *vik,* meaning bay or creek, the place where the raiders' ships lay hidden. A Viking was a person from one of these creeks or bays.

The Vikings loved fighting and showed no mercy to their foes, often taking even children as slaves. But they believed in equality among themselves, and when they were asked, "Who is your leader?" they would proudly answer, "We are all equals!" Vikings also wanted to die in battle and be buried in their ships.

Some Viking ships have been found in ancient burial places. The ships are beautiful, swift, and graceful, but they are quite small, and it would take great courage to sail in them. The Vikings must have been brave and hardy to travel so far on unknown seas in such small ships.

During the time of the Vikings, missionaries were bringing the Christian faith to many countries. Saint Ansgar of the Franks brought Christianity to Sweden. Many of his men were driven away or murdered, but they kept trying to spread their ideas. Finally King Olaf Skötkonung agreed to accept Christian beliefs and was baptized. But many people fought against the new religion. Ministers even had to put metal walls around their pulpits to prevent themselves from being hit by spears and arrows.

Although the Vikings treated each other as equals, the Swedes kept squabbling among themselves. Two families claimed the right to rule the country. A leader from one of them invited his enemies to a party, threw them in jail, and left them to starve.

In 1397 Queen Margaret brought Sweden, Denmark, and Norway together. This important time was called the period of the Three Crowns. Today there are still three crowns on the Swedish coat of arms.

Because Margaret was bossy, the Swedes accepted her son for their next king. A cruel ruler, he had those who disagreed with him killed—eighty-two people in one day alone! The Swedes called this terrible time the Stockholm Bloodbath.

Among those beheaded were relatives of a noble named Gustavus Vasa. He escaped from prison and made his way to Sweden, hiding from the king's men. Once he hid in a wagonload of grain. When the soldiers stopped the wagon and thrust their spears into the grain, he did not cry out, even though he was wounded. Later a woman lowered him out the window of a house while the king's men banged on its door. Another family put him in their cellar, placing their Christmas beer on top of its door to fool the soldiers. Their stone house is still standing.

On Christmas Day, Gustavus spoke to the farmers of the province of Dalarna at Mora, begging them to help him drive out the cruel king. But the men were too afraid of the king to join him. Disheartened, he left the town in the cold and the snow.

The men of Dalarna had always been bold and steadfast. After Gustavus left, they thought about what he had said. Seeing that he was honest and fearless and willing to lead them to freedom, they decided to fight for Gustavus and sent two of their fastest skiers after him. "Dalarna is ready," the messengers said.

With the farmers of Dalarna at his side, Gustavus drove the Danes out of Sweden. Because he brought freedom to Sweden, he is known as the father of his country.

Gustavus ruled Sweden wisely and built a strong government. Under his leadership, Sweden broke away from the Roman Catholic church and established the Lutheran church as its state church.

Out of love for their lively, attractive king, with his huge red beard, the people elected his son Eric for their next ruler. Eric started out well, but he soon became suspicious and cruel. He tried to marry a foreign princess, but Queen Elizabeth of England, Mary Queen of Scots, and several French and German princesses all refused him. They did send their pictures to him, though, and these are hanging in Gripsholm Castle, along with Eric's own portrait. His bearded face is long and sad.

Since no princess would have him, Eric married a soldier's daughter. Little by little, he became insane, doing frightening, unreasonable things, like stabbing prisoners in their cells and running about in the woods, howling like an animal. He also threw his brother in jail. Some people said Eric's head had been

Gustavus Vasa ruled Sweden from 1523 to 1560. Under his leadership, the Swedes gained their independence from Denmark.

cracked one time when he was tossed in a blanket.

Finally the Swedes made his brother king instead. Eric died in the same cell where his brother had been held, after eating poisoned pea soup. Since his death, it has been a Swedish custom to eat pea soup on Thursday.

Another great Vasa king was Gustavus Adolphus. A big, cheerful man with long golden hair, he was only seventeen when he came to the throne. But he had worked hard to make himself ready. He could speak eight languages, and he understood warfare better than any man of his time.

Gustavus made the law treat everyone fairly. He said that if any judge did things just to please the king (or some other person), the king would have him punished.

When the Danes invaded Sweden, Gustavus led his people to war, soon making his enemies sorry. The Swedes won battle after battle under their Golden Lion of the North. His soldiers loved him because he shared their dangers and hardships. Under his leadership Sweden took over land that is now part of Russia, Poland, and Germany.

A wise ruler, Gustavus Adolphus planned to make Sweden strong and great. One of his ideas was to build what later became the Göta Canal as a short-cut for ships across Sweden. But in the 1600s, no one knew how to make water run uphill, and the canal could not be built.

Gustavus also wanted Sweden to have a large navy, and one special ship was called the *Vasa* in his honor. Dazzlingly beautiful, it had a lion for a figurehead, and each of its sixty-four cannons had a lion's head on its red firing door.

When the ship was ready, it sailed proudly out into the harbor, flags flying. Everyone in the court was thrilled at the sight of the mighty ship. Suddenly, a light wind came up. And then to the surprise and horror of all, the ship turned over and sank.

The *Vasa* lay on the bottom of the sea for three hundred years. Not long ago, it was raised from its watery grave, and it can be seen today in a Swedish museum in Stockholm.

When Gustavus was killed in battle in Germany, the Swedes were heartbroken. They brought him back to Sweden for a great funeral, but they refused to let any foreign visitors come. They didn't want the world to see how poor they were.

The crown passed to Gustavus's daughter Christina. She called herself king, wore men's clothes, and kept a pet lion. Under her rule Sweden became very poor. Later she gave up the throne and went to live in Rome.

Sweden did not have another great ruler until

Carl XII came to power. Since he was only fifteen when he became king, other countries thought the time was right to try to conquer Sweden. But the boy-king and his soldiers defeated Sweden's foes and later invaded Russia. There the Russians won a great victory over the Swedes.

The young king was loved by his soldiers, who gladly followed him into battle and made Sweden one of the strongest powers in Europe for a time. But Carl XII was killed in a battle in Norway, and his wars lost Sweden all the territory it had gained in Gustavus Adolphus's time. Even so, his courage and skill made him Sweden's greatest hero.

By the 1800s Sweden was no longer a great power. It was ruled by an old king who had no children. To make sure there would be another king after he died, the Swedes invited a French general, Jean Bernadotte, to be their crown prince. The feeble old king adopted this grown-up Frenchman as his own son. Sweden's new prince had to learn to speak Swedish!

Bernadotte was an honest man and a loyal leader. Although he was called the regent, or acting ruler, he really ran the country. He had been the friend of France's Emperor Napoleon, but he fought against the French to defend Sweden. As a result of the wars with France, Sweden gained control of Norway.

Carl XII, who was only fifteen when he became king, is Sweden's greatest hero.

Bernadotte was later elected King Carl XIV, and all of Sweden's kings have since come from his family. They are able, democratic leaders who have kept Sweden at peace for 175 years. The Bernadottes may be French, but their hearts are Swedish.

As time went on workers wanted more say in how the government was run, and nobles and church leaders lost some of their importance. To give the common people of Sweden more rights, the old Riksdag, Sweden's parliament, was changed. In the new one, there was still a powerful body of wealthy men and nobles, but there was also a group of lawmakers who were elected by the farmers.

When crop failures and overcrowding brought starvation to Sweden, many working people left for America. The Riksdag then passed new laws to make life easier for peasants. The parliament also set aside old laws that kept trade in the towns, and that made it hard for commoners to own land or learn a craft. From this beginning, Swedish laws have become more and more helpful to the common people. Today Sweden provides many benefits for all its citizens— health insurance, pensions, free lunches, and medical care.

As time passed, more people moved away from their farms and into towns, where they began to work in factories. Sweden gradually changed from a land of farms to a nation of industries. In time, workers formed strong labor unions, each made up of the people who work in one industry. These unions supported the Social Democratic Party in the Riksdag.

For nearly fifty years, starting in the late 1920s, the Social Democratic Party headed Sweden's elected governments. The Social Democrats and the heads of industries worked together to make life better for all Swedes. During this time the Riksdag passed many of the laws that provide benefits for ordinary people. Industries had a free hand to make the profits needed to support the government's generous programs. As long as Sweden's companies remained healthy, this system worked well.

In recent years, though, Sweden's industries have been hard hit by the economic slump that has hurt many countries throughout the world. As a result, many Swedish workers have lost their jobs. To protest these job layoffs, in May 1980 labor unions organized the first general strike in seventy years. This strike, along with a lack of demand for Swedish products, created problems for many businesses. The government has tried to help by giving money to troubled companies and retraining workers for new jobs. But in order to do these things, it has had to borrow a great deal of money.

Such hard times have caused Swedes to wonder if

they can afford to keep all their generous government programs. To help make things better, industry leaders want labor unions to accept a three-year wage freeze. The labor unions, on the other hand, want money set aside to buy shares of companies for workers. Meanwhile, the government has plans to increase taxes to raise the money it needs to continue to aid industry. No one has all the answers to Sweden's current problems. Most Swedes, however, are willing to work together to meet the challenge facing their country.

Today Sweden's government is a mixture of old and new. The king remains, although he does not lead his people in wars. Laws are made by the Riksdag and carried out by the cabinet. The cabinet also appoints a governor for each county, but elected officials deal with all local matters. Because there is so much government help, taxes are very high. Nearly half of a Swede's wages goes to pay taxes.

But the new Sweden does not forget the past. In Stockholm's Skansen Park, old buildings show what life was like long ago. A cottage like the ones built in the 1500s has a wooden beam just a foot inside its door. Called the Pauper's Beam, it marked the spot past which beggars could not come. The Friend's Beam, in the middle of the cottage, could not be passed except by invited guests. Last of all was the

Dressed in traditional folk costumes, these modern-day Swedes show visitors to Skansen Park, Stockholm's famous open-air museum, what a country wedding was like.

Master's Beam, two feet from the far wall. The law could not take any man who stood beyond it. There are also other old buildings in the park from later centuries that show how the common people lived.

Swedes are proud of their history and keep it very much alive. They have preserved old burial mounds that are filled with the bones of ancient kings. They give tours of castles that are scattered throughout the country. And their museums display pictures and statues of great leaders and famous events. The little horse ridden by Gustavus Adolphus and the clothes he wore when he was killed are also exhibited. And markers show the stone on which Gustavus Vasa stood to plead with the men of Dalarna and the cell where his son Eric died. They also identify the spring where Olaf Skötkonung was baptized, along with the place where he is buried.

The Swedes are not certain what the future holds for their country. But like the singers and the story-tellers of the ancient sagas, they do not want the past to be forgotten. And so they have made sure that their famous ships and old homes, as well as the stories of their great kings and heroes, will live on.

4. Magic, Make-Believe, Ghosts, and Old Gods

If you lived in Sweden a hundred years ago, you would have wanted a *tomte. A tomte* (or *tomtar,* if you were lucky enough to have more than one) was the best thing a farmer could have.

We would call him a brownie or a good-luck spirit. He was a little old man, no bigger than a six-year-old child. Sometimes he was even smaller, the size of your hand. He liked people. If you were the right kind of person, he would make his home under your floor or in a chest. Sometimes he would live in a barn.

Tomten was a busy creature who hated dirt and laziness. He would not stay if your house was messy or your work sloppy. In a home where things were well taken care of, tomten would do his part. At night he would do the work the farmer had been unable to finish during the day. Once in a while the farmer might hear tomten talking to the animals. Often he could find the little old man's wee tracks or small gifts he had left.

Hardly anyone ever saw the tomtar, although someone born on Sunday had a better chance than most people. But once you had seen the tiny creatures, you could join them in their midnight dances.

And dance they did, on moonlit nights. They loved music, and there was one song they ab-so-lute-ly couldn't resist. Any tomte who heard this song just *had* to dance and couldn't stop unless it was played backwards, or the fiddle strings were cut. When country people saw stripes in the dewy grass, they said the tomtar had been dancing there.

Tomten did not ask for much. He liked to play with your animals, ride in your hay wagon, and be appreciated. You could thank him with a bowl of rice pudding on Christmas Eve. Oh, a tomte was a great help.

But there were evil spirits, too. These were the trolls, or dwarfs. They, too, were little old men, but they had many bad ways. Though they had heaps of gold, they wore old grey clothes. They lived under the hills or in caves, with their kings and treasures.

The trolls were ugly looking. They had long, warty, crooked noses and fierce scowls on their faces. Carrying heavy sacks of gold also made them hump-backed. And they were always cross.

If food was missing from your pantry, you knew the trolls had taken it. They stole other things, too. Their worst deed was to trade their ugly children for human boys or girls. They would keep the human children in their troll hill, while the youngsters' parents tried to train a bad-tempered troll child to behave. As long as the children were not afraid of the trolls, they would not be harmed. They could play with the trolls and not be hurt.

Perhaps because they lived underground, trolls were skilled with metals. If you left a piece of iron and a shilling at the troll's hill, he would make whatever you wanted from the iron and keep the money.

But trolls did not like noise, and thunder really frightened them. In fact, you could drive them away by making loud sounds. Saying the name of God or marking a cross on something would make it safe from trolls. A piece of steel across the doorway would keep them out. There was even a special doctor, called *klocka män,* who was supposed to be able to cure sickness caused by trolls. People tried to be careful not to make the trolls angry.

Spirits of another sort dwelt in all the lakes and streams, where they could be heard singing sad songs. Using their music, they tried to attract humans to come to them. This was the only way they could be set free.

Every castle had (and sometimes still has) its own spook, or *spöken,* which haunted the place where it was said to have died. Most of these ghosts were thought to be the spirits of people who were murdered or who lived unhappy lives.

Certain objects were also thought to have special powers. The bridal crown of Ebba, Gustavus Adolphus's love, was supposed to bring special blessings to the girls who wore it at their weddings.

There were witches, too. Like witches everywhere, they rode about at night on brooms. Yet they not only carried cats, but also coffeepots! They gathered at a make-believe mountain, Bläkulla, at Eastertime. People shot firecrackers on the night before Easter in order to scare the witches away.

Some magical creatures living in the world were never seen. Each child—not just princes and princesses—had a fairy godmother. These fairies were the *nornir*. They brought gifts to the newborn babies and helped them all their lives.

Other spirits made their homes in the woods. People who went into the woods and did not return were taken away by the *skogsrå*, or wood trolls. The *maran*, a creature that gave people bad dreams, was a human by day and a wolf at night.

Nisses, necks, mermaids, and mermen were about at all times, and people needed to know just how to keep from making them angry and casting spells. Sacrificing a black lamb on Thursday to *Ström-karl* would bring the gift of music. To curtsy or bow to the new moon on New Year's would bring good luck for the next year.

Many tales about trolls and spirits come down to us through the *Edda,* a collection of very old poems. The name Edda meant grandmother. It was given to the poems because, like a grandmother, they were full of wisdom.

A number of the stories in the Edda came from old *skalds,* or singers. These people made up songs about heroic deeds and great events and sang them for kings and nobles in their castles. Finally some of the songs were written down. They tell us of things that people in ancient times believed. Sometimes these things are true, and sometimes they are not.

One of the oldest tales concerns the hero Beowulf. He was a fearless Goth with a giant's strength. When the monster Grendel kept raiding the lands of the Danish king Hrothgar, no one could stop him. Grendel came to the king's castle, killing his men and dragging them off to his cave. Beowulf overcame the evil beast with his bare hands. Scholars believe that Beowulf really did live and do brave deeds.

Before the Christians came to Sweden, the people believed that many gods ruled the world. Telling stories about these gods was their way of explaining things they didn't understand.

We are surprised to learn that people today can trace their families back to these old gods. Perhaps they were not gods at all, but leaders. When these leaders were involved in something unusual, people may have given them credit for having magical powers and soon looked on them as gods.

Odin (who is sometimes called Woden) was the chief of the gods and their father, too. Swedes saw him as an old, bearded man with one eye, who rode a white horse. He had traded his other eye for the gift of wisdom. Knowledge was important to Odin. He wounded himself and hung from the tree named Yggdrasil in order to learn the magic secret of writing.

The human beings Odin liked best were warriors. He watched battles, looking to see which men were brave. When heroes were killed, he sent beautiful maidens to go and get them. These maidens, called Valkyrie, swooped down over the battlefields and carried the heroes to Valhalla. Here they would be waited upon forever by beautiful girls and do nothing but drink mead and brag about their great deeds.

Odin's wife was named Frigg. She seemed to have no powers of her own. Most of the other important gods were their children. Thor was the god of thunder—fierce, short-tempered, and very strong. Frey was a gentler god. He brought the sunshine and the rain. It was he who made the crops grow and gave the farmers a good harvest. His sister Freyja was the goddess of love. Kindest of all, and most beautiful, was Balder, the god of justice.

Another important god was Loki, the evil son of a giant. He was always making trouble. There was no reason for most of his pranks—he just wanted to be mean. Though he was always caught and punished, this did not seem to stop him.

Many stories are told of the gods' doings. One tells how Loki cut off the golden hair of Sif, Thor's wife, while she slept. Thor was angry enough to kill him, but Loki promised that he would bring Sif new hair. It would be made of real gold, he said, and would grow like her other hair. Then he went to the dwarfs for help. They not only made the hair, but two other magical things that he could give to the other gods as well. Loki was so pleased with their work that he bragged about it to the dwarf Brock, betting his head that no one could make anything finer.

Brock took up the challenge. With his help, his brother Sindri made three different magical gifts. Then they brought them to the gods at Asgard.

One of Loki's gifts was the ship *Skidbladni*, which he gave to Frey. It was so small it would fit inside a purse, but when needed could grow large enough to carry hundreds of warriors with their weapons. Wherever the ship sailed, the wind would be behind it. To Odin, Loki gave the spear called Gugner, which always hit its mark when it was thrown in battle. And of course Sif got her new hair.

Then Brock gave his gifts. Odin received the golden ring Drupner, which would drop nine rings just as beautiful as itself every ninth night. For Frey he had a golden boar that could run through air or water, by day or by night, giving its own light. Best of all was the hammer for Thor. When he seized it and swung it around his head, thunder growled and lightning flashed. And if the hammer were thrown at a troll, it would always strike its mark.

Loki lost his bet, and he should have lost his head. But Brock could not catch him, because Loki had shoes that would run through air and water. The dwarf then asked Thor to help. Thor caught Loki for him, but that crafty fellow pointed out that although his head could be cut off, Brock could not touch his neck. As a result, all the dwarf could do was sew Loki's bragging mouth shut.

Perhaps you think these old gods have nothing to do with you. Did you know that some days of the week are named after them? Wednesday is Odin's or Woden's day. Tuesday is named for Tieu, a less important god. Thursday is for Thor's day, and Friday for Frey's day. The old gods have very little to say about your life, but you often speak of them.

Even while Vikings still roamed the seas, the Swedes gave up their old gods. Swedish children no longer believe in trolls and tomtar either, any more than you do. But they do enjoy stories of magic. *The Wonderful Adventures of Nils* tells of a boy's magical adventures. Once he flew on the back of a goose, and he even saw a tomte. You may have read Astrid Lindgren's stories about Pippi Longstocking. This little girl was so strong that she threw robbers up on the roof of her house. And when she went somewhere with her horse, *she* carried *him.*

Science has chased away the old spirits, ghosts, and gods. We do not believe much about things we cannot see. Yet when something happens, we want to know what caused it.

The early people of Sweden also wanted to understand their world. However, when they could not find the reason behind something, they said it was caused by a god or spirit. It is a little bit sad that when they needed help, they had nowhere to turn. They hoped to make their lives better through the magic of gods, trolls, tomtar, and other beings.

5. Fun Times

In Sweden, not a month goes by without a holiday. Some of these holidays are very old celebrations, and customs have grown up about them. In fact, on holidays Swedes do things as they have been done for hundreds of years.

Christmas is a joyful season. It begins long ahead of time, on Saint Lucia's Day, December 13. On this day, a young girl in a family is awakened at dawn. She is dressed in a white robe, and a crown of candles is placed on her head. Then she brings breakfast to her family. There are special buns served at this meal, flavored with cardamom, the fruit of a pleasant smelling herb.

Lucia Day has become a big holiday. Because clubs and factories choose their own Lucias, there are thousands of these maidens of light. There are parades and parties in schools and offices. Everyone starts to get ready for Christmas.

Before Christmas Day arrives, the house is cleaned from top to bottom, and gingerbread is made, just as it was years ago. Sheaves of wheat are placed outdoors for the birds. Holiday breads are baked and hams are prepared.

One of Sweden's biggest festivals is held every year on December 13 for Saint Lucia, "the Queen of Light." Thousands of young women dress in white robes and wear a crown of candles as part of the celebration.

Candles are everywhere, because part of the Christmas celebration is for the return of light. The darkest day of the year is December 22, after which the sun will start to return. Candles are put on graves in the churchyards, too.

These kindergarten-age children in Göteborg, Sweden, are learning how to make candles, which play an important role in the Christmas celebration.

Of course, there is a Christmas tree, decorated with old-fashioned ornaments made of straw. The holiday is a Christian celebration, but straw goats standing for the old god Thor are seen everywhere.

Presents are part of Christmas, too. In olden times, people gave funny gifts called *julklappar* as a joke. The family would hear a rap *(klappa)* on the door. When it opened, nothing would be there but a humorous gift. Other secret presents were put in odd places by Jul Tomten, the Christmas elf. When the father handed out the Christmas gifts, he often dressed like Jul Tomten, perhaps putting on a long beard. The children would bring him rice pudding.

People eat special foods at Christmas. Swedes love *lutefisk,* a dried, split cod, which is soaked and boiled and then eaten with melted butter or cream sauce. Another custom is *doppa i grytan,* which means to dip bread in the water used to boil the Christmas ham. People eat this bread to remind themselves that long ago poor people had no other food. In addition, everyone is so busy that there is often no time to fix a proper meal.

Many kinds of sweets are made for the holiday. There are *kringle* (pastrylike cream puffs), *sandbak-kelse* (sand tarts), *krumkake* (which are rolled and crisp), *rommegrot* (a cream pudding), and *lingonber-ries* (like cranberries).

There are many things for children to do at Christmastime. They help with the preparations for the holiday, decorating the house. They put colored paper stars that have light shining through them in the windows. When the Christmas tree is up, the children do special dances around it. Sometimes there are "star boys." They dress in white robes and carry a staff with a star on its tip. They go about singing carols or acting out stories. One may dress like Thor's goat.

The Christmas season has grown longer and longer. People now celebrate Advent, the coming of Christmas. Parks, streets, and stores are decorated, and for a month before Christmas, a candle is lit in churches and homes each Sunday, until four have been lit. People also send Christmas cards and do many other things done at this season in other parts of the world. An Advent calendar, with little windows to be opened each day, helps even the youngest child know when Christmas will come. But the celebration does not end on Christmas Day. It goes on until Saint Knut's Day, January 13.

New Year's is part of the same celebration, though it is not connected with the church at all. People make sure that they look at the New Year's Eve sunset because there is an old saying that it shows what the next year's weather will be like. There are

Making cookies is one of the many activities that children take part in at Christmastime.

also parties and family gatherings at New Year's time. Children pour melted lead into basins of water, where it spreads into odd shapes. Called "fortunes," the form the shapes take shows something in your future. A gun, a bell, a shoe—whatever it is, you will meet it in the next year.

Crowds gather in the streets on New Year's Eve. At the stroke of midnight, factory whistles blow, churches ring their bells, and people shoot off firecrackers.

The next day, all is quiet and serious, and people pay special visits of respect. Anyone who wishes may even visit the king, and write his or her name in the visitor's book.

In Skansen Park, the world's largest open-air museum, there is a solemn service. Someone reads the poem "Ring Out, Wild Bells" by Alfred Tennyson, and bells all over the city ring out. People go to church and give each other New Year's cards.

Easter is another church holiday. There are old customs connected with it that are fun, too. Everyone eats hard-boiled eggs, which are sometimes hidden on the lawn by the Easter bunny. The eggs may have pictures from the Bible on them, but they are not always painted or decorated. In olden times, Easter was the end of Lent, during which people gave up many foods to honor Christ's sorrows. It was also the time when hens, having given no eggs for months, began to lay again. Having eggs was a special treat people looked forward to.

It is still too cold for flowers at Eastertime, and so people bring birch twigs mixed with brightly colored feathers into their homes. When placed in water, the buds of the twigs swell and open, showing the first green of spring.

Easter is also the time of witches. Long ago people believed that witches gathered on Good Friday, and so they built fires on the night before Easter to scare them away. Boys still haul barrels of tar to the top of a hill, making a huge bonfire. Girls become Easter hags, smearing soot on their faces and dressing in old clothes. With shawls over their heads, they knock on doors. In exchange for a drawing, they are given a small treat.

People shoot firecrackers to scare the witches away. They dance all night around the bonfires, waiting for the Easter sunrise. Then they go to church, sometimes in their old costumes.

Later in the spring, there are celebrations for students who are finishing their schooling. Some of these celebrations are based on customs once connected with Examination Day. On this day tests were given to determine who could go on to higher schooling.

Today students no longer have to take these final examinations. Their interests and abilities plus the marks they earn in ninth grade determine what kind of higher school they will attend. But in some places, students who are graduating from a higher school carry on the old customs just for fun. They put on white caps and ride home from school in a tub or wheelbarrow. Sometimes bands play, and people march and sing. At home there is a special dinner for family and friends, and presents, too!

Midsummer is the biggest holiday of all, and, next to Christmas, the happiest. It used to be held on June 24, but now it is celebrated on the weekend closest to that date. Long before Christian times, it was a joyful event, because it is the day when the sun shines the longest. For northern people, this day has always been a very important time.

Flowers and birch leaves are everywhere at Midsummer. They decorate homes, fences, cars, and boats. People not only hang them on their hats, but carry them.

During Midsummer a tall tree is chosen, cut down, and brought to the center of the town. This is the maypole (*majstång*). It is decorated with birch twigs, flowers, and long streamers. Then it is set up, and the dancing begins. In rainbow skirts and old-fashioned costumes, young people dance all night long. Of course, at this time of year there is really no night at all. Violins and accordions furnish the music, and people sing. The songs and dances are centuries old.

The next day everyone goes to church, dressed in their finest clothes. In Dalarna, people row across the lake to their worship service in a long church boat.

The raising of the maypole begins Sweden's Midsummer Festival.

Even the boat is decorated with birch twigs, and the people in it sing old hymns as they come.

Sweden has other holidays that are church festivals. One is Shrove Tuesday, the day before Lent begins. Lent was once a time for fasting, and people wanted to have one big feast before it began. Often there was a party, with everyone wearing a costume and mask. At one such party, one of Sweden's kings died after eating the special dessert. This dessert is a bun filled with almonds and covered with whipped cream that floats in a dish of warm milk. It does not sound very delicious, but Swedes still eat it on Shrove Tuesday.

Though Sweden has been a Lutheran country for over four hundred years, a special day honors the Virgin Mary, the mother of Christ. Called Lady Day, it comes on the Sunday nearest March 25. Long ago, on the night before this day, people went to bed without any light in order to show that from then on daylight would last until bedtime. Some people believed that cranes brought the light back from the south in their beaks. They also thought the cranes brought gifts. Today, in some parts of Sweden, children hang their stockings by their beds on Crane Eve, so that the birds can fill them with gifts. For a special treat, the children eat waffles.

Walpurgis Day is another exciting time. It honors

the beginning of warm weather, which is so important to Sweden. Special bonfires are lit, and singing goes on all hours of the night. Students have customs of their own. In Uppsala, at exactly 3:00 in the afternoon, they put on their student caps—the white caps with blue bands that they wear to show that they are students. Then they gather in groups and sing sad songs. The bells of the castle at Uppsala ring, too.

One old custom on Walpurgis Day was egg-singing. When eggs were hard to get, young people would visit farms. In exchange for a song, they would be given eggs.

Walpurgis Day is April 30. The next day, May 1, is quieter. It is a time of important meetings and special events. On this day farmers take cattle out to pasture for the first time, and people all over Sweden visit parks and country homes. The king and his family also visit Djurgården, a huge animal park in Stockholm. Their subjects know about this visit and come to the park to cheer for them. Sweden has set aside this happy day as its Labor Day.

On Ascension Day, people once again go to the country. They hope they will hear the cuckoo sing for the first time. It is a day for picnics, as well as the first official day for fishing.

Whitsunday, or Pentecost, is another day for outings. Most of these outings are to celebrate con-

Special bonfires are lit on Walpurgis Day, which marks the beginning of the warm weather season in Sweden.

firmation, a ceremony held when people become full members of the church. This day is another time for gifts and flowers. But Swedes use any excuse to go to the country.

In August comes a time that is not really a holiday, but which still involves feasting. It has to do with a small lobsterlike creature called the crayfish. Swedish law says that crayfish cannot be caught before August 7. But when this day arrives, the crayfish parties begin. There are fireworks, fancy displays, and music to make them more fun. The parties go on for several weeks because the little sea creatures are so delicious that no one gets tired of eating them.

Food has been the reason for another special day. It all started in Skåne. Farmers there held meetings on Saint Martin's Day and often ate goose at their dinners. Because Saint Martin, the Bishop of Tours, was believed to have had a great interest in cooking, other Swedes began to follow the farmers' practice. After a time, eating a goose dinner on the bishop's day spread throughout Sweden. In Skåne, it is often a day off from work and school.

Another holiday is All Saints' Day, the day after Halloween. It is like Memorial Day in the United States. Graves are decorated with candles and flowers, as Swedes honor those who died in battle to bring them freedom.

This holiday should include Gustavus Adolphus, but Sweden loved him so much that he has been honored with a day of his own. On November 6, the day of his death, flags fly in his honor, and people eat special rolls called Gustav Adolf buns. These buns are decorated with a mixture of almonds, egg whites, and sugar called marzipan that is made into the shape of the king's head.

Sweden has a Mother's Day, a Children's Day, and many other holidays much like those in North America. Birthdays are also special times, though not long ago "name days" were celebrated instead. Each date on the calendar had been given a name—Sara, Erik, Johanna, and so on. When the day with your name occurred, you were given a party. Everyone named Gerda celebrated on the same day, as did everyone named Carl. Name days made it easy for your friends to have a celebration for you. They didn't have to remember your birthday.

Sweden has a name day of its own. Several kings have been named Gustavus or Gustav. The sixth of June, which has the name of Gustav, is celebrated in the king's honor. This custom began nearly two hundred years ago, and the day is now Sweden's national birthday, or Flag Day. Parades are held, and the Swedish flag is given to clubs and groups. Sweden has been at peace for so long that it is not an exciting day. Like our Flag Day, it sometimes goes by without much notice.

If you have counted them, you can see that Swedish children have many holidays. Some of them—Christmas, New Year's, Walpurgis, Easter, and Midsummer—are celebrated two days in a row. There is not much danger of the Swedes' lives being all work and no play.

6. *The Swedes at Home*

Sweden seems to be a wonderful place for children. Everything is done to make them healthy and happy. School, food, clothing, parks, books, sports, travel, doctors, dentists—all are free to those who need them.

All children have the same opportunities. They go to the same schools and live in the same way. They have the same chance for a college education and the same amount of time for a vacation. When parents must be away, there is even a hotel just for children to stay in.

Moreover, parents are forbidden to spank their children. That is the law. Another law that is being discussed says that neglected or abused children may ask for new parents.

With so many laws to make people equal, you might expect them to be very much alike. Of course, this isn't so. Swedes are as different from one another as North Americans. Still, there are some ways which are common throughout Sweden. If we know about these things, it will help us understand the Swedish people.

Sweden, as you know, is a nation of factories

rather than farms. Because of this, most Swedes are town or city people. Most of them live in apartments. In a cold country, central heating makes an apartment more comfortable than a house. So many people want apartments that there is often a waiting line to get into one.

The government has set up many rules about apartments. It says how large their rooms must be and how much they may cost. For this reason, apart-

Most Swedes live in towns or cities and have their homes in apartment buildings.

ments tend to be very much alike. The home of a rich family is not much different from that of a family with a small income.

Most apartments are light, bright, modern homes in fairly new buildings. Inside, the rooms are spotlessly clean and shining. Floors are made of highly polished wood, with small bright rugs. Wood is used for tables, chairs, and other furniture, too. The Swedish love of clean, plain lines has given its name to simple designs—"Swedish modern." Fancy curlicues or bulky pieces of furniture do not fit well in Swedish homes.

A Swede is not likely to stuff his room with pictures or small articles. Decorations are neat and well chosen, and glass or wood ornaments made in Sweden are popular. Sometimes there are Scandinavian rya rugs or bright woven hangings. Almost every home has fresh flowers.

The kitchens have the most modern equipment. Swedes have more appliances than any other people in Europe, including such devices as stoves, refrigerators, freezers, and dishwashers.

A small fraction of Swedes live in the country. Farm homes are modern, too, though they may not look it. Some have stood for centuries, but most have had modern plumbing for years. Water power has made it easy for homes all over the country to have

Kitchens, like other rooms in modern Swedish apartments, are brightly lit and simply designed.

electricity. Long before rural areas in North America had electric power, Sweden's farms were modern, and the farmers now have machines to do the hard work. Because fewer people live on farms, however, many of the little wooden farm cottages have become summer homes for city families.

In the north of Sweden we find another kind of home. The Lapps who live here are not truly Swedes at all. Many of them still follow the reindeer, and they need homes that can easily be moved. They must travel for two weeks to drive the animals from summer pasture to winter range. During this time, the home must be packed up every morning. That night it will be set up in a new place. As a result, the best shelter for the reindeer herders is a skin tent.

The herders cannot carry many things with them as they travel. They take only the tools that they must have and depend on the reindeer to meet most of their needs. Their homes and their clothes are made from reindeer hides. In addition, reindeer pull the sleds filled with their goods. The animals also provide them with meat and with milk to make cheese. Along with wild berries, these things are their main foods. The Lapps' money comes from the reindeer, too. The animals' meat is sold in stores and restaurants in the south of Sweden, where it is considered a special treat.

In Lapland many people live in large tents made from reindeer hides.

Not all the Lapps move about with their herds. In fact, many of them live in small settlements and have wooden houses. In winter they travel about by snowmobile, and they shop in supermarkets. In most ways, they live like Swedes in the southern provinces.

Reindeer are the chief source of the Lapps' income. Each year the vast herds must be rounded up so that some of the animals can be sold to meat marketers.

Neither the Lapps nor the Swedes have large families. Among the Swedes, only one family in fifteen has more than four people in it. Most households are made up of a mother, father, and one or two children. In three out of four homes, both parents work. The state provides day-care centers so that small children can be well cared for.

Children have a part in family life, just as you do. In the cities they may do errands or help with household chores. Farm boys and girls usually have outdoor work. In summer they care for gardens, help with haying, and work with animals.

During the day, a typical family's home is empty. Very few people have servants, both parents often work, and children are in school or at day-care centers. Workers are usually on the job by eight o'clock in the morning. Nearly all bring a lunch of sandwiches and milk to work with them. Children, of course, will be given a hot meal at their school or care center.

Meals in Sweden follow a pattern. Breakfast is a light meal, often toast, or hardtack, with cheese. *Filmjölk* or *filbunke* is eaten in some homes, perhaps with corn flakes. This food is much like yogurt, and may be served with fruit or with cinnamon and sugar. Bread and rolls are common breakfast foods. Some families eat porridge, and a few may have herring or boiled eggs.

Most Swedish couples have only one or two children. This family of four is relaxing after breakfast, which is usually a light meal of toast, cereal, eggs, or fish.

The next main meal, *middag,* is a large one. It is usually eaten some time between 4:00 and 6:00 P.M. At this meal there will be cooked food, with a dish such as meatballs or fish. The evening meal, served any time between seven o'clock and midnight, will be a lighter one.

One food the Swedes eat day after day is fish. There are several kinds of fish, and Swedes like them all. The fish may be pickled, smoked, fried, boiled, or made into a soup or a salad. Both Baltic herring and North Sea herring, which differ somewhat, are quite popular. Cod, which is often dried, is another favorite.

Swedes are famous for the *smörgåsbord.* This word means a meal of sandwiches, but it is far more than that. A smörgåsbord is a table loaded with as many as forty different foods. Guests take their plates and serve themselves a small amount of each food that they want. Besides the ever-present fish, there are several kinds of cold meats, cheeses, hard-boiled eggs, many kinds of pickles, and breads of all sorts. Some are crisp breads no thicker than a cracker—rye crisp is a favorite. Others are puffy rolls. Many hot dishes are included, and there are always salads and potatoes.

One Swedish favorite is called *fågelbo,* or bird's nest. It is made from a raw egg in a nest of chopped raw meat or fish. This dish may sound odd to us, but Swedes often laugh when they are told that Americans enjoy corn on the cob. To them, corn is food only for livestock.

You shouldn't think that the Swedes dislike American foods, however. They do, although they may change them somewhat. A Swedish hot dog is likely to be a sausage wrapped in a pancake.

Some Swedish foods have been popular for a

More than forty different kinds of food may be served at a Swedish smörgåsbord.

long time. *Lutefisk* (codfish soaked in lye) is a winter treat. Swedes are also fond of *köttbullar* (small spicy meatballs in a cream gravy), *getost* (goat cheese), and jellied *strömming* (Baltic herring). Nowadays not many housewives have time to make old-fashioned dishes like Janssen's Temptation (potatoes with anchovies). But the old standby holiday cookies like *spritz,* squeezed through a cookie press, or *sandbakkelse,* baked in a little pleated mold, are enjoyed everywhere.

Bread is a mainstay of the Swede's diet. The big wheels of *knäkkebröd* and hardtack date back to the olden times. Then bread was baked only once a year and stored on poles strung across the ceiling.

Desserts range from old-fashioned rose hip soup, made from the seed pods of rose bushes, to ice cream. Lingonberries and cloudberries are Swedish specialties.

In most Swedish homes Sunday dinner is served in courses, using the best dishes and silverware. The first course is likely to be boiled potatoes, with butter and parsley, followed by herring. The next course might be meat and potatoes. The meal is formal and takes a long time.

A party is also likely to be very formal. Guests are careful to be exactly on time—not early, and certainly *never* late. If they arrive at the building a few minutes ahead of time, they usually wait in the street before they ring the doorbell. It is considered proper to bring flowers to the hostess.

Strangers in Sweden notice how polite Swedes are. Everyone is greeted courteously, and "Thank you" is said over and over. After a meal guests say, "Thank you for the food." The next day, they say, "Thank you for yesterday." They also usually send flowers to show their appreciation. They may even telephone to say thank you again.

On her part, the hostess tries to show that she feels honored at having guests. When she offers food, she says, *Var så god,* which means, "Be so kind as to eat some of this." If the guests eat her food, she thinks that she has been done a favor. Swedes are very warm and thoughtful and go to great trouble for their guests.

When the food is served, people eat with both a knife and a fork. The fork is held in the left hand, and used for bringing food to the mouth. The right hand holds the knife, which is used to cut and push the food.

The Swedes take great pleasure in eating. In their free time they also enjoy the same activities that North Americans do. Television is found in most homes, with programs often coming from the United States. The Swedes also watch the same movies and

listen to the same songs that are popular in this continent. American and Canadian rock stars are popular
there, just as Abba, from Sweden, is enjoyed here.
Many Swedish young people belong to the Girl
Scouts and Boy Scouts, and they have often had
North American scouts as guests. Swedes have a close
bond with the United States, since nearly every family
has a relative living there.

In Sweden, as in North America, no two families
are quite the same. Yet because of government programs, Swedish families have much the same life-
style. Government grants help people to deal with
most family problems. People who are ill, handi-
capped, or unable to work receive money to live on.
The country's health insurance system helps to pay
for doctor and dental bills and to provide medicine
and hospital care. Newlyweds are given money to
start their home. When a baby is born, its parents
receive a cash allowance to care for it. Artists, writers,
and mothers-to-be are aided by government support.
And by law there is a paid vacation for all workers,
including housewives.

Sweden's idea is that a healthy, secure life for
each person makes a better country for everyone. We
do not know if this idea would work everywhere. We
do know that it has been successful in Sweden for
nearly fifty years.

Some Swedish Recipes

As you have read in this chapter, the Swedes eat many different kinds of foods. Would you like to know how to prepare some of them? Let's start with *tjack pannkaka*, which is an egg pancake.

Tjack Pannkaka
   (Serves 6)

   4 eggs
   1-1/2 cups flour
   1/2 teaspoon salt
   1-1/2 cups milk
   1/4 cup butter

Beat eggs lightly, add flour and salt, and stir in milk, a little at a time, to make batter. Put the butter in a 9x12 cake pan. Place the pan over heat until the butter melts. Pour the batter into the pan.

Bake the pancake at 400° F. for 30 minutes. Remove it from the pan and let it stand for a few minutes. Serve it with jelly, sauce, or berries, and sausages.

Köttbullar
  (Serves 6)

Swedish meatballs, called köttbullar, are often served at middag, the main meal of the day.

 1/2 cup bread crumbs (or stuffing mix)
 1 cup canned milk
 1 pound ground beef
 1/4 cup chopped onion
 1 egg
 1/2 teaspoon nutmeg or allspice
 2 teaspoons salt
 1/8 teaspoon pepper
 2 teaspoons flour
 1 cup hot water

Soak the bread crumbs in 1/2 cup of canned milk. Mix the ground beef, onion, egg, nutmeg (or allspice), salt, and pepper into the crumbs. Shape this mixture into small balls no larger than a walnut. Fry the balls in butter until they are browned on all sides. Take them out of the pan and stir the flour into the juice that remains. Add the other 1/2 cup of the canned milk and the cup of hot water. Heat this mixture until it is a thick sauce. Put the meatballs and sauce into a baking dish, and cover the dish.

Bake the meatballs at 350° F. for 15 minutes. Remove the dish and serve.

Julekaka
  (Makes 1 loaf)

Julekaka is a Christmas bread. Here is the way to make it.

   1 loaf frozen raisin bread dough, thawed
   1/4 teaspoon cardamom
   1/4 teaspoon cinnamon
   1/2 cup candied fruit

Roll out the raisin bread dough into a big flat circle about 1/2 inch thick. Sprinkle on the cardamom, cinnamon, and candied fruit. Roll the dough up again, pull it into a long roll, and place it on a greased cookie sheet. Let the dough stand in a warm place until it is soft and fat—about 1 hour.

Bake the bread at 350° F. for 30 to 40 minutes. Remove the bread from the oven and let it cool.

Rommegrot
  (Serves 6)

In the old country, rommegrot, or cream pudding, is made with rich cream. When cream is used, however, the dish must be cooked carefully to keep it from scorching, and the butter that forms must be poured off. Here is an easier way to make the pudding and have it taste the same.

  1/2 stick margarine (Swedes would use butter)
  1/3 cup flour
  2 cups milk (or a pint of half-and-half)
  1 teaspoon sugar

In a heavy saucepan, melt the margarine and then stir in the flour. Keep stirring while you add the milk and sugar. Cook over medium heat. When the pudding starts to thicken, pour it into serving dishes. (If you want to, put a raisin in one dish before you pour the rommegrot. The person who gets the raisin will be lucky all year.) Serve with cinnamon and sugar.

7. *School Is for Life*

In Sweden, school is serious. Children not only attend school because they have to, but because they want to prepare themselves for the future.

The law says that children must start school when they are seven. Most of them, however, will have had some schooling before this. There are kindergartens, day-care centers, and nursery schools in all parts of Sweden.

In the year of their seventh birthday, children start primary school, or *grundskola*. The first year is much the same as first grade in North American schools. There is one teacher for a roomful of pupils. Yet the room is not crowded because there are usually not more than twenty children to a class. When the classes are small, the teachers have more of a chance to deal with students who need help.

In most cases, as children grow older, their eyes and hands can work together more easily to master reading and writing. As a result, it is unusual for Swedish children to have great difficulty with these subjects in their first year of school. Besides, Swedish is somewhat easier to learn than English because each letter in the language looks and sounds the same whenever it appears in a word. Long ago, children learned to read just by knowing the alphabet. Once they knew the sound of a letter, they could easily identify words.

Swedish classrooms are much like those in North America. Children sit at tables or desks, and their teacher may be a man or a woman. Students and teachers work and talk together in a friendly, relaxed way. After all, a teacher is a special friend who is trying to help a child learn. People respect educators, and many hope that their own children will become teachers.

Some of the pupils' names might seem strange to you. Asta or Inga, Sigrid or Ingrid, Gunhild, Borghild, Kristin, Katrin, Signe, Mai, Hildur, and Liv are common, traditional names for girls. Boys are often named Sven, Rolf, Einar, Ingmar, Birger, Axel, Lars, Tegner, Dag, or Johan. But it is not unusual to find children named Barbara, Ellen, or Anne-Marie, as well as Dennis, Robert, or Norman. Swedish parents often give their children English names, just as people in North America name their children Eric, Carl, Karen, or Ida.

In the first three grades, the children learn reading and writing, along with a little mathematics, language, science, and art. When a pupil begins third grade, something new is added—English. Swedish children study English for at least three years. Sometimes a Swedish sixth-grader can write English as well as an American the same age.

The Swedish pupil can do so well because English and Swedish are related languages. *Son, man, hand, arm*, and *finger* are the same in English and Swedish. *Kaka* for cake, *kan* for can, *kaffe* for coffee, *kopp* for cup, *fader* for father, and *moder* for mother are easy to understand. Besides, the Swedes get used to English from television programs, movies, and comics that come to them from the United States. (See Appendix B, p. 135 to learn more about Swedish words.)

Mathematics is also very much the same as in the United States, except for measures. Swedish children have never had to learn about pounds and ounces, feet and yards, quarts and gallons. For years, their country has used the metric system, in which things are measured in units of tens. Soon this system will be used in the United States, and Americans will not think it odd to hear that a girl weighs 35 kilograms (77 pounds) and that her shoes are size 25 centimeters (10 inches).

Gymnastics, a very important subject, is taught to everyone. People at home can also keep in shape because music for gymnastic exercises is broadcast throughout Sweden.

After six years of grundskola, children are ready

All Swedish youngsters are required to complete nine years of basic schooling. Most of them then continue their education for at least two more years.

for secondary school. From this time on, they have a separate teacher for each subject, instead of learning everything from just one teacher. The children begin to choose special classes that will help them in later life. At the same time, they start learning a third language. This time it will probably be French or German.

There will be another new thing in seventh grade—vocational counseling. A trained teacher will give tests to all the children to help them decide what they are best fitted to work at. Then they will choose extra classes to help them in his field. Those students who plan to be nurses or doctors will take science courses. If art is their main interest, they will look for classes in it. Of course, students may change their minds. If they have chosen hard math courses, for example, they may decide that they would rather study great books. In this case they are allowed to take different classes. Still, it is important to plan what one will do in the world in seventh grade.

In the eighth grade, students go one step farther, working at the kind of job they have planned. Someone who plans to be a nurse will work in a hospital, bringing water and meals to the patients or cheering up sick children. A student who thinks of a teaching or coaching career will work with younger children. Future mechanics may work in a garage.

This on-the-job training helps students prepare

for ninth grade, when they make a final choice about courses. They can choose from over twenty programs grouped into three areas: arts and social studies, science and technical studies, economic and commercial studies. No program is regarded as being especially for girls or for boys. Students may take whatever interests them, whatever will help them prepare for a job or a career.

After nine years of school, most students are sixteen years old. Now they may leave school and go to work if they wish. But Swedish children seldom do.

Students never drop out of school because they can't afford to go on. In Sweden, all education is free. There are free books, free paper, and free hot lunches. In addition, free transportation and free clothing are given to those who need it. Besides these things, an allowance is paid to the parents of each child under the age of sixteen. This allowance can continue up to age twenty if the child stays in school beyond ninth grade.

Not too long ago, there was something that all students dreaded at the end of the ninth grade: the final examination. This big test was given at the end of basic schooling to determine whether students had learned all they were supposed to know. Only those students who passed it were allowed to go on to higher schools. Some parts of the test required spoken answers, and other parts written ones.

At the time of testing, everyone was anxious—not just the students, but fathers, mothers, and grandparents. They would gather in the schoolyard and wait to hear if their children had passed. If they passed, everyone was excited, and there were presents and parties to celebrate their success.

Some of these customs are still observed, but people do not have to worry about the tests themselves anymore. Now anyone can go on to the university if he or she has finished secondary school with a certain grade point average. As a result, children try hard to be the best students in their classes. They know that getting high marks is very important to their future. Indeed, their marks are a part of their personal records and are used to judge them all through life. Do you know what your marks were three years ago? In Sweden you would not forget. They are too important.

After ninth grade is over, the stream of children going to school divides. Some of them will spend the next three or four years in vocational school. This kind of school teaches them the skills that are needed for a certain job. They can study to be a cook, a farmhand, a typist, or some other kind of worker. Along with their special subjects, the students must also study what are called general subjects—art and science—and learn another foreign language.

Another group of children will go to continuation school, which lasts for two years. It, too, is planned to help students learn skills for jobs. However, it does not require them to take as many general subjects.

Students who show a talent in some field may have a chance to attend the special schools run by certain Swedish companies. Then they will be trained to work for those companies.

Young people who plan to go to a university must attend a *gymnasium*. In Sweden this word does not mean a large room used for playing indoor sports. It is what North Americans would call senior high school. Only those students who have finished ninth grade with very high marks may go to this school. For three years they will study hard subjects—social studies, economics, science, and art. And they must learn another foreign language. All this work is to get them ready for the university. Only when it is finished are they called "students."

In Sweden, a "student" is someone who is ready for college, as in the case of gymnasium graduate. In a way, though, young people in the gymnasium have already begun college because their courses are very advanced. In fact, they learn as much in their studies as North Americans do after two years of college. A Swedish "student" is also likely to be twenty or twenty-one years old, nearly the same age as a North

American college graduate. It is an old tradition that "students" may wear a special cap. The Swedes think it is an honor to be educated, and so this cap is worn with dress clothes.

Here again, people do not need money if they wish to continue their education. The university is free, and the government will even lend students money to live on if they need it.

Those people who somehow missed their chance to get an education when they were children also receive help from the government. Long ago, folk high schools (*folkhogskolorna*) were started for grown-ups who wanted to learn. One of them, Söranger Folk School, is over one hundred years old. The government provides money to support these schools and encourages people to attend them.

Then there are adult training schools. People who would like to change jobs, or who are faced with losing them because of new machines, can take free retraining courses. Now that people are coming to live in Sweden from other countries, free courses in Swedish and job training have been set up for them. Classes in handwork and hobbies are also available to all adults who are interested in them. Making things at home is an old tradition in Sweden, and so teachers help older people to learn such things as wood carving and rug weaving. By studying good design, these people can see how to make more beautiful objects.

Besides the schools, there are other ways for people to learn things. Study circles bring greater knowledge to Swedes everywhere. In them, adults join together to study a subject they would like to understand better. Those adults who wish to study alone can take lessons by mail or through television courses. All of these lessons are free. For the Lapps, who must move about, there is a special moveable school that goes where they go. Older boys and girls in Lapp families can also take lessons through television or by mail. No wonder there is almost no one in Sweden who cannot read or write. School is never over!

Some young people further their education through travel, often combining their trips with work. Girls may go to England or the United States and work in someone's home. Taking a trip like this gives them a chance to practice English and to see another kind of life. Boys do not often get this kind of chance, but those who work on ships may see other countries.

Young men also do some traveling when they become soldiers. Every man in Sweden between eighteen and forty-seven must serve at least ten months in the armed forces. A few young men choose to make a career in the army, navy, or air force.

Although Sweden's educational system is quite

modern, interest in learning goes back many centuries. In fact, Swedes had a kind of writing of their own thousands of years ago. Messages called *runes* were carved in stones or written on sheepskin (vellum). Hundreds of old rune stones may be seen in Sweden today.

The ancient Swedes wrote in characters called runes. This rune stone at Rök in Östergötland county contains the largest runic message known in the world.

The nation's most valuable treasure is the *Codex Argenteus,* a Latin copy of the Bible written in letters of silver on purple parchment. This beautiful book has an interesting history. Once, long ago, some pages disappeared from it. They could not be found, and it was feared that they were gone forever. After some years, the watchman who had been entrusted with guarding the book died. On his deathbed, he gave back the pages. It was he who had stolen them. Now the book is locked up every night at the library in Uppsala where it is kept. Visitors to the library can see it during the daytime, though.

Queen Gunilla thought learning was so important that in 1588 she left money for the ringing of a special bell. Every year since then, the Uppsala castle bell has rung at six o'clock in the morning and at nine o'clock at night. Queen Gunilla thought that scholars should spend the fifteen hours between these ringings in study. You could do quite a lot of homework in that time.

Parents encourage their children to do their best in school. Many still follow an old custom based on the saying, *Tuppen varpte,* which means, "The rooster laid an egg." Of course, no one believed that roosters really laid eggs. However, to reward children for doing their lessons, mothers and fathers would hide a piece of flat candy in a schoolbook. When the children reached that page, the saying came true. The "rooster" had "laid" a gift for the hardworking students.

Today school in Sweden is not like it was yester-day. It has changed, and it will keep on changing. Boys and girls are now being made ready for life as it may be in the year 2020. Their parents and teachers believe that happiness and good fortune will come only to people who have a key to open the doors of the future. If learning is that key, then the young Swedes should be well prepared to enter the next century.

8. Sports and Games

School vacation lasts from June until the middle of August. The weather is warm then, and it is a good time for family holidays. Swedes are known as "sun worshipers" because they spend so much of the summer out of doors. Whole familes go mountain climbing, sailing on the ocean, or sunning on the beach. And most of them don't have to go far from home because many places for outings or vacations are close to where they live.

No place in Sweden is far from water. Thousands of lakes and rivers, as well as miles of ocean beaches, make it a perfect land for swimming. Learning to swim is important, both for safety and for fun. Not everyone is a good swimmer, but only a very few people cannot swim at all. Each year, Sweden, Finland, and Norway give swimming tests to all children. The country which has the most children who can pass the tests is the winner. Children who cannot swim one year want to do better the next in order to put their country on top. Besides, swimming is fun for everyone.

Another favorite summer sport is boating. It would be hard to find a Swede who has never had a

Swedes don't have to travel far to find a place to sail, swim, or sunbathe. In Stockholm, pictured here, people can do all three things in the center of the city!

boat ride. Years ago, boating was a good way to travel because lakes and rivers made good highways. People living on one side of a lake often went to a church on the other side by traveling in large boats that held thirty people.

Crossing a lake in this manner is no longer the best way to get to church. However, church boat races are still part of the fun of the Midsummer Festival. The large boats carry twenty rowers and a number of passengers dressed in their best clothes. The rowers speed across the lake at Mora as fast as they can, trying to beat each other. Both the passengers and the people standing on the banks of the lake cheer for their "team." Some people get wet! It is all part of the celebration.

Besides the large boats, there are many smaller craft. Some are rowboats that hold only one person. Beautiful modern motorboats go up and down the water-roads formed by rivers, lakes, and canals. Since nearly everyone can swim, even children who are quite young are allowed to handle small boats.

People who love sailing anchor their boats on the large lakes or the ocean. Sailboats have been used in Sweden since earliest times, and Viking ships crossed many strange seas, using both sails and oars. With a sail to catch the wind, boats could go faster and farther than other ships, with much less work.

Many boats in Sweden are built just for sailing. They are sleek, light, and slender. With wind filling their sails, they slip swiftly and silently through the water. The large lakes are dotted with these ships, and their colorful sails are a beautiful sight among the islands of the Swedish coast. Often, they race each other. Boys and girls can go sailing in smaller boats. A square of cloth fastened to a mast will turn any boat into a wind-powered sailboat.

Swedes take to the water in still another way. They have adopted the canoe, a fast, light craft invented long ago by American Indians. It is perfect for traveling long distances over the water with some speed. Now that canoes are made of aluminum or plastic, they have become popular in Sweden. Canoe tours are mapped out, just as they are in your country. Some are slow and easy, for those who want to see the landscape. Others are down fast, tricky streams that have foaming rapids. These trips are for skillful paddlers. International canoe championship races are also held in Sweden.

Swedes who enjoy waterskiing can find plenty of places for this activity. The tricks that expert water-skiers can do also make the sport fun to watch. Dare-devil skiers strap kites to their backs and sail into the sky as the motorboat that pulls them along speeds across the water. When the boat slows down, they float back onto the water.

Summer is also the time for lying on the beach. The warm weather lasts for only a few months, and so people flock to sandy shores to sun themselves beside the ocean.

For the outdoor-minded Swedes, summer is likewise the best season for camping. To make exploring easy, there are youth hostels all over Sweden. These shelters are especially meant for young people, but anyone can use them. For a very small sum, travelers can spend the night at a hostel, where they will find places to sleep and cook, as well as firewood ready to use. For this reason, campers do not need to bring much with them. But they must observe one rule: they must leave the campsite clean and gather wood for the next camper. In this way, the youth hostel is always ready, and each new camper feels welcome and expected.

Hiking, or backpacking, is another popular activity because most places in Sweden are not long distances apart. Many people hike through the forests that cover much of the land. Others travel to wilderness areas that are not far from the cities.

Boys and girls with knapsacks on their backs and staffs in their hands are a common sight in Sweden. Sometimes groups of them tour Lapland in this way. By going far from the traveled roads, they can see more of the old Lapland ways.

A trip through Lapland that many people enjoy can be taken on the Royal Hiking Trail, which leads south from Abisko to Kvikkjokk. It is 135 kilometers (81 miles) long altogether. But travelers do not hike this distance nonstop—there are overnight huts every 10 kilometers (6 miles). In the olden days, when distance was measured differently, the trip did not sound very far at all—only about 13 miles. One Swedish mile, however, was the same as 6 North American miles!

Orienteering is a new sport. With only a compass to show them the way to go, people must find their way over a course. They must follow directions that tell them which way to go and how far. These directions may lead them through a forest, across a stream, or past a waterfall. The contest is to see who can get to the end of the course without getting lost.

For those people who do not have much time to spend, trips can be made by bicycle. Travelers can also go by "train-home." A train takes them to interesting places and serves as their hotel on the way. After the train has brought them near to the trail they want to follow, they can start their hike.

Fishing in the fast streams of Sweden used to be a famous sport. People came from England and Germany for the fun of catching salmon and other fish. It is not so popular now because the "acid rain" produced by factories in northern Europe has hurt the fish. This form of pollution is caused by the burning of fossil fuels, especially coal. The waste products of burning rise into the air, are changed into acid particles, and fall into rivers, lakes, and streams with raindrops or snowflakes. In time, enough acid builds up in these waters to kill the fish. Still, there are many places in northern and eastern Sweden where the fishing is good. The government is working on plans to stop acid rain, but it will need the help of the countries from which the pollution comes.

Among Swedes who like active sports, tennis is popular. Many years ago, newspapers often showed pictures of King Gustav V playing tennis. Perhaps you have heard of Bjorn Borg, Sweden's famous tennis star. He has won many world tennis titles.

Golf is played in many places in Sweden. One course in Lapland is quite unusual. During June and July, when the sun never sets for weeks, players who start their game at midnight can play all "night" in full daylight. When their game is over, they go home to breakfast.

Another popular sport is football, but it is not the same game that North Americans play. "Association Football" means soccer, the favorite team sport in Sweden. Almost everyone plays soccer, and there are even special championship teams. Perhaps you know something about this game, since it is spreading across the United States.

Soccer is somewhat like football, but the tackling is not so rough. It is played on a rectangular field, measuring 100 to 130 yards (91 to 119 meters) long and 50 to 100 yards (46 to 91 meters) wide, with a goal at each end. The goal is a space 8 yards (7.3 meters) wide and 8 feet (2.4 meters) high, guarded by a goalkeeper. Players use a round ball that looks like a patchwork basketball.

Each team has eleven players, who try to put the ball in the other team's goal. The team that scores the most goals wins the game. At the start of the game, each team lines up on its half of the field. Play begins when the ball, placed at midfield, is kicked.

Except for the two goalkeepers, players cannot use their hands to move or stop the ball. They can only bump or kick it. The game is divided into two forty-five minute halves, and there are no time-outs. Players can only rest during a short period between the halves.

Compared to soccer, folk dancing may not sound like a sport, but it, too, takes good wind and strong legs. Dancers need to practice for hours to learn their steps and to match their movements to the music.

During the summer festivals, folk dancing is done in colorful costumes, and it is fun for everyone. People of all ages dress in the clothes that were worn years ago. Each part of the country has its own costumes, different from any other region. The dances are old, too.

The songs and actions of the dancers tell stories. One dance shows boys trying to coax girls to go up to the mountain. Another one, the weaver's dance, moves streams of people in and out to the music. Dances are beautiful to watch and fun to do. The dancers look so happy, everyone wants to join in.

After the summer, there is a hunting season during September and October. Sweden's largest forest animal is the elk, a big, mooselike creature. If elk herds grew without control, the animals would soon use up all their food. Then they would starve to death. As a result, each year some elk must be hunted so that others may live.

Winter sports are as popular as summer games. Sweden's oldest winter sport is skiing. Long before the rest of the world found out how much fun skiing could be, Swedes were skimming over the snow on boards. It was a fast way to travel over snowy plains and mountains. In ancient times, skis were nine feet long and six inches wide. The old kings used skis to help their soldiers in wartime. In fact, Magnus the Good defeated the Roman legions with ski troops. Other kings used skis for their messengers and scouts.

Today skis are much shorter, lighter, and narrower, and almost every Swede is at home on them. All winter long villages hold weekly skiing contests, and students have a "ski vacation" from school. Some

The Vasa Loppet is Sweden's most famous cross-country ski race. Each year thousands of people participate in it.

people even go to Lapland in May and June to ski, after the snow has melted in other parts of Sweden.

The ski races are for everybody. In cross-country races, hundreds of people of all ages line up at the starting line. The most famous Swedish ski race is the Vasa Loppet. (*Loppet* means ski race.) It is held on the first Sunday in March. On this day long ago, skiers raced from Mora to Salun to catch up with Gustavus Vasa. Now racers ski over the same trail. Each year, eight thousand people ski this fifty-five miles (88 kilometers).

Downhill skiing, which requires wider, heavier skis, is popular, too. Skiers go down steep hills as fast

Ski jumping is a popular Swedish sport. The most skilled jumpers leap into space from hills that are nearly 300 feet (90 meters) high.

as they can without falling. There are ski runs and chair lifts for downhill skiing all through the mountain backbone that divides Sweden from Norway.

Ski jumping takes greater skill and daring, as well as longer and wider skis. Long ago, when skis were the only means of traveling through the snowy, roadless mountains, people sometimes came to steep cliffs or wide crevasses. The only way to cross these spaces was by jumping. And so the skiers developed a special skill that was almost like flying.

Today ski jumpers whiz down an artificial hill, which is often a ramp, jutting out over a slope. When skiers reach the end of the ramp, they leap out into space, leaning far forward to cut into the wind. As they rise into the air, their skis become like a kite and let them float gently to the ground. The whole jump is breathtaking to watch. Only experts try the hundred-foot (thirty-meter) towers, but there are many smaller hills with jumps for beginners.

Because skiing is so popular, it is not surprising that some of Sweden's skiers have become famous. In the 1980 Olympic games, Gustaf Wassberg won a gold medal in cross-country ski events. Ingmar Stenmark, who won two gold medals, is considered to be the greatest downhill skier in the world. He lives and practices in the north of Sweden.

Skating is popular in Sweden, too. Besides speed

skating and figure skating, there is sail skating. In this sport, skaters wear a kitelike sail across their backs. When the wind blows into this sail, they go zooming over the ice at thrilling speeds.

Other skaters play ice hockey. It is Sweden's favorite team sport in the winter. The country's national hockey team, known as *Tre Kronor* (Three Crowns), is world famous. In the 1980 Olympic Games, this team won a bronze medal. The Swedes also enjoy bandy, a kind of ice hockey played with a ball instead of a puck.

Playing on the ice is also fun for people who don't skate. On many frozen lakes big brothers and sisters push little ones about in a chair on runners. Boats can have skates, too. These ice boats dip and whirl across the glassy surface of the frozen water.

Curling is another sport that has many players. In this old Scottish game, an oval-shaped stone or piece of iron is slid across the ice. As this stone moves along, several members of the curling team sweep the ice ahead of the object to make it go farther. At the 1980 Olympics, Sweden's national curling team tied with the United States for fourth place in this sport.

Indoors, gymnastic exercises can be enjoyed by everyone. Children have gymnastics classes at school, while people in homes and businesses take part in the exercises by listening to the radio. Though this activity is rather new to North America, it is quite old in Sweden. People there were doing the exercises in the eighteenth century.

Swimming, boating, hiking, fishing, soccer, skiing, skating, and folk dancing are only a few of the sports and games Swedes enjoy. The Swedish Sports Federation has divisions for fifty-six different sports, and contests are held in all of them. But winning is not the most important thing to the Swedes. They know that not everyone can be a champion. The contests are held to make people do their best. By seeing others perform, they can learn how to improve.

The Swedes like sports for a number of reasons. They think that games and exercises build strong bodies, teach valuable skills, and bring people together. But most of all, Swedes like sports because they are fun.

9. Swedes in America

More than a hundred years ago, the Northern and Southern states of America were at war with each other. The Confederate states of the South had an ironclad ship called the *Virginia*. Covered by plates of armor, no cannon shot could pierce its sides. One by one it began to destroy the Union ships of the North.

President Lincoln's men were afraid. They thought the South would sink all their wooden ships. All they had to fight the *Virginia* was a small, new ship called the *Monitor*. It had been designed by John Ericcson, a Swedish immigrant. The *Monitor* did not look like an ordinary ship. Instead, it was low to the water like a raft and had a gun turret like a tank. Because of this round turret, it could turn its guns in any direction.

On March 9, 1862, the *Monitor* sailed out against the *Virginia*. The big, proud, Confederate ship could do nothing against the small odd contraption that attacked from all sides. It sailed away and never returned. President Lincoln's fleet was safe. A Swedish immigrant had helped to save the United States Navy.

John Ericcson was only one of many Swedes who

came to America to seek a better life. All of them helped to change their new land.

The idea of Swedes starting a colony in America came from Gustavus Adolphus. In 1638 he sent a group to America in the ship *Kalmar Nyckel.* They landed in what is now Delaware, where they built Fort Christina, named after the king's daughter. Their commander in the new country was Peter Minuit.

The first Swedes in America were peaceful farmers. They became friendly with the Delaware Indians and started missions and trading centers. As a result, there was no fighting between the Indians and the settlers of New Sweden. One settler, Per Lindstrom, wrote a book about the Delaware Indians and their customs.

As more people came, the colony in Delaware grew. In 1643 they pushed up into Pennsylvania, seeking more land for homes and farms. You can still find traces of their settlement at Chester. But when Sweden lost its world power, it also lost its colonies in America. In 1655, the Dutch, who had a colony in what is now New York, took them.

For around two hundred years after they lost their colony in Delaware to the Dutch, the Swedes stayed at home. It took a time of dreadful trouble to send them out again. In 1848, and again in 1868 and

1869, there were terrible famines in Sweden. Food crops failed, and people were forced to eat whatever they could find. They were so hungry that they used leaves, nuts, and bark for bread. Many people—especially children—died from lack of food. As a result, thousands of families left Sweden and braved a terrible journey to a new land. Weeks of sailing the stormy Atlantic brought them to America.

Other emigrants had different reasons for leaving their homeland. Life in Sweden was very hard during the nineteenth century. Rich people owned most of the land. In addition, many farmers could not pay their debts because their farms were so small. Though they worked hard, they could not raise enough food to sell. Other Swedes had to work hard for cruel masters, getting almost no wages. Children who had no parents were sold as servants.

Life was also difficult because taxes were heavy and laws were harsh. For example, young men were made to serve in the army. Likewise, people could not worship as they wished, and if they did not agree with the church rulers, they were punished.

Despite the hard times, more people were learning to read, and there were often stories about America in their books and newspapers. Many Swedes came to believe that it was a country where they could find both freedom and room to live.

A group of Swedes from Östergötland settled in
Iowa in 1845. The next year, some people who did not
want to belong to the Lutheran church, Sweden's
state church, came to Bishop Hill, Illinois. They were
seeking in America the freedoms they did not have in
the old country: freedom from hard masters and freedom to worship.

Wild stories spread through Sweden about this
far-off land. Gold was said to be lying about on the
ground for anyone to pick up. There were supposed
to be so many horses that you could easily catch a
hundred of them a day. Other stories claimed that
everyone was equal, that the land had no stones, and
that a pig in the New World lived as well as a lord in
Sweden.

Some of these stories were true, but some were
not. Yet because of them, thousands of Swedes
decided to travel to America. Making the trip cost
fifty dollars—a great sum in those days—and the only
way to go was in wooden sailing ships.

The voyage was a journey of terrible hardships.
The travelers were crowded into the hold of the ship.
Families huddled together in groups, but there were
no separate rooms. Only a small trap door let in light
and air. In this dark, foul place, many people became
sick, and dreadful diseases spread among them. On
some voyages, nearly all of the passengers died.

Sometimes ships sank at sea, and everyone on board perished. Even people who were well suffered from lack of fresh food. Only the very brave dared to make the trip to America.

Yet even for the brave, the trip was a sad and lonesome experience. It meant saying good-bye forever to their old home and friends, since news of their dear ones would not reach them often in the New World. In addition, they knew that they would have many troubles to face even when they reached America. There would still be hundreds of miles of land travel ahead of them.

Arriving in the new country, they had little money left. Yet since they could not bring much with them, they needed to buy many things. Their clothes, for example, were worn-out from the three-month-long voyage. They needed help, but did not know how to ask for it. American money, language, and customs were all new to them. Often, wicked people pretended to help them, but cheated them instead. However, there were good people, too. And in the end, most Swedes did find a better life in spite of their problems.

Land was still plentiful in America, and it was good, fertile soil. The emigrants could have much larger farms than they had owned in Sweden. The new Americans worked hard and learned new ways.

Many Swedish immigrants came to Minnesota, where their first homes were plain-looking log cabins.

Their children went to American schools and began to study English. The fathers and mothers learned, too. By the light of kerosene lamps, in log cabins, the children taught their parents to speak English. The parents still read Swedish-language newspapers to learn what was going on in the world, but America was their homeland now.

The newcomers wrote to their friends and relatives in faraway Sweden. Some sent money to people in the old country. Many of these people packed an "America chest" and sailed to the new land. As word spread of the freedoms in America, more and more immigrants followed. The Swedes had a word for the excitement: "America fever."

When transatlantic steamships were built, America became easier to reach. Nearly one person out of four in Sweden left for the New World. Travelers today find that nearly every Swede they meet has an American relative. Minnesota Day is celebrated in Växjö, a town in southern Sweden. Swedish-American days are held in Stockholm every August. People who gather at these festivals are honoring the many brave, hardworking people who brought the heritage of Sweden to the new land.

Swedish Americans now try to observe many old ways from their Swedish heritage. In Mora, Minnesota, there is a large, carved, red horse, like the famous Dala horse of Sweden. Many American cities and towns have Swedish festivals, where folk dancing is done in bright costumes as in the old country. Swedes in America often gather at Christmas to eat lutefisk and *lefse*, or potato bread. At Lindstrom, Minnesota, there is a statue of a Swedish immigrant.

Some Swedish Americans helped to make the world a better place. You know about John Ericcson. Besides the *Monitor,* he built a special hot air engine. Most important, he invented the screw propeller, which drives steamships. America honored him for his work. When he died, an American battleship carried his body back to Sweden for burial.

Another inventor was Frank Mossberg, who held

200 patents for such things as roller bearings and fog signals. Mossberg even made an electric car that would run for sixty miles (ninety-six kilometers) on one battery charge. Liss Peterson helped develop transistors for Bell Telephone Company. Alfred Stromberg and Androv Carlson invented a telephone which worked so well that people who used it would not only hear the speaker, but a dog barking outdoors as well. Perhaps you have heard of Stromberg-Carlson, the company they founded.

Sweden has provided the United States with heroes, too. The Confederates called Roger Hanson "Old Flintlock"; he died in the battle of Murfreesboro, Tennessee. A Civil War tombstone honors John Hammond, who founded the town of Hammond, Louisiana. Most exciting of all is Charles A. Lindbergh, the young "Lone Eagle," who was the first person to fly alone across the Atlantic Ocean.

Since Swedes often came to America for better government, it is not surprising that many famous political leaders are Swedish Americans. Three of America's presidents had Swedish ancestors: William Henry Harrison, Benjamin Harrison, and Franklin Roosevelt. John Morton, signer of the Declaration of Independence, was also of Swedish descent. It was his vote that tipped the balance towards gaining freedom from England when the issue of independence was being weighed in the Continental Congress.

Since 1899, Minnesota has had ten Swedish governors. One of them, John A. Johnson, became his family's breadwinner when he was just thirteen. He was about to be nominated for president when he died. Another Minnesotan, Orville Freeman, became secretary of agriculture. Abraham Fornander became a judge in Hawaii and is also famous for his books on Hawaiian history and folklore. Earl Warren was chief justice of the U.S. Supreme Court.

The list of Swedish business leaders is enormous. Celotex was begun by Gustav Dahlberg. Charles Walgreen, beginning as a shoe clerk, started a drugstore in Chicago; now Walgreen drugs are found all over the United States. Ray Edwin Powell, at one time a page boy in the U.S. Congress, became the pioneer leader of aluminum manufacturing in Canada. Peter Waller's fifteen factories make gloves of all kinds. Some are fireproof, some are made for barbwire, and some even have one finger. The Matson line of steamships was founded by a Swede. An Arizona lumberjack, Carl Eric Wickman, started the Greyhound Bus Lines, beginning with a small motorcar in Hibbing, Minnesota.

Swedish-American scientists are headed by Glenn T. Seaborg, who shared the Nobel Prize in chemistry with Edwin M. McMillan in 1951. He has worked on nuclear energy projects and been head of the Atomic Energy Commission. The 1936 Nobel Prize in physics was won by Carl Anderson for discovering the positron, a particle of matter. The chemist Bengt Kjellgren discovered beryllium, a light metal needed in the manufacture of special steel.

Swedish Americans have also made a mark in literature, art, and entertainment. The most famous poet is Carl Sandburg. Before becoming a writer, he worked as a milk driver, a bootblack, a soldier, a farmer, and a salesman. He was even a hobo. Painters include Gustaf Tenggren, whose pictures appear in many children's books. He is honored for the movie *Snow White*. Gustavus Hesselius, who came to America in 1712, is known as the father of American painting. The light and graceful statues of the sculptor Carl Milles are displayed in both America and Sweden. The Ice Follies, the first ice show, was the brainchild of Roy Shipstad and Oscar Johnson. The famous "skating horse" formed by two skaters was their idea.

Some notable Swedish women who have entertained American audiences are Jenny Lind, Greta Garbo, and Ingrid Bergman. Lind, known as the Swedish Nightingale for her beautiful soprano voice, made a memorable singing tour through the United

*Greta Garbo became one of America's most famous actresses.
In 1933 she starred in* Queen Christina, *an MGM film.*

States from 1850 to 1852. Garbo came to America in 1925, acted in both silent movies and sound films, and in time became an American citizen. As mysterious as some of the women she played in her pictures, she retired from filmaking at the height of her career. Ingrid Bergman made her first American picture in 1939. Afterwards she acted in a number of other important films and won an Academy Award.

What a long list this is! Yet these are only a few of the Swedes who have contributed to America's way of life. Indeed, there are many fine citizens of Swedish ancestry who have helped to build this nation.

The people of Sweden are proud of these citizens, and they have maintained close ties with their relatives in the United States. However, they want to share their heritage with all North Americans. Perhaps now that you have read something about their country, you will want to learn more about the Swedes. There are Swedish consulates in many North American cities which can provide you with more information. If you want to travel in Sweden, the Scandinavian National Tourist Offices can help you plan a trip.

One day you may meet a Swede. If you do, remember to shake hands and to say thank you for any courtesy or kindness that is shown to you. These things should help you begin a friendship that may well last for a lifetime.

Appendix A

Swedish Consulates in the United States and Canada

The Swedish Consulates want to help North Americans understand Swedish life. They will try to answer your questions and can provide you with a variety of educational materials. Contact the consulate that serves your state or province for more information.

U.S. Consulates

Chicago, Illinois
Swedish Consulate General
333 North Michigan Avenue, Suite 2301
Chicago, Illinois 60601
Phone (312) 726-9868

Alabama, Arkansas, Illinois, Indiana, Iowa, Kansas, Kentucky, Louisiana, Michigan, Mississippi, Missouri, Nebraska, New Mexico, Ohio, Oklahoma, Tennessee

Los Angeles, California
    Swedish Consulate General
    10960 Wilshire Boulevard, Suite 304
    Los Angeles, California 90024
    Phone (213) 473-0901

The counties of: San Luis Obispo, Kern, Santa Barbara, Los Angeles, Ventura, San Bernardino, Orange, Riverside, Imperial, San Diego

The states of: Hawaii, Arizona

Minneapolis, Minnesota
    Swedish Consulate General
    615 Peavey Building
    730 Second Avenue South
    P.O. Box 2186
    Minneapolis, Minnesota 55402
    Phone (612) 375-0572

Colorado, Minnesota, Montana, North Dakota, South Dakota, Texas, Wisconsin, Wyoming

New York, New York
    Swedish Consulate General
    825 Third Avenue
    New York, New York 10022
    Phone (212) 751-5900

Connecticut, Delaware, Florida, Georgia, Maine, Maryland, Massachusetts, New Hampshire, New Jersey, New York, North Carolina, Pennsylvania, Rhode Island, South Carolina, Vermont, Virginia, West Virginia, District of Columbia, Puerto Rico, Saint Thomas.

San Francisco, California
Swedish Consulate General
1960 Jackson Street
San Francisco, California 94109
Phone (415) 775-6104

Alaska, California (except the counties that belong to the Consulate General in Los Angeles), Idaho, Nevada, Oregon, Utah, Washington

Canadian Consulates

Montreal, Quebec
Swedish Consulate General
1155 Dorchester Boulevard West, Suite 800
Montreal, Quebec H3B 2H7
Phone (514) 866-4019

Toronto, Ontario
　　Swedish Consulate General
　　920 Yonge Street, Suite 820
　　Toronto, Ontario M4W 3C7
　　Phone (416) 967-7172

Vancouver, British Columbia
　　Swedish Consulate General
　　207 Hastings Street West, Suite 1105
　　Vancouver, British Columbia V6B 1H7
　　Phone (604) 684-5971

Other Sources of Information

American Swedish Institute
2600 Park Avenue
Minneapolis, Minnesota 55407

Swedish National Tourist Office
3600 Wilshire Boulevard
Los Angeles, California 90010

Swedish National Tourist Office
75 Rockefeller Plaza
New York, New York 10019

Appendix B

Swedish Words

There would not be room to tell you all of the rules for pronouncing Swedish words, but here are some of them:

1. *g* sometimes has the sound of the *g* in *game,* as in *gamla* (old), but in a few words it sounds like *j.* For example, *korg* (basket) is said as if it were spelled *korj. g* can also sound like *y.* Göteborg (a city) would be said Yötebory. In some cases *g* is silent. *Några* (some) sounds like *nora.*
2. *j* is pronounced as we would say *y. Ja* (yes) is said *yah*; *mjolk* (milk) is *myolk.*
3. *qu* is pronounced *kv.* Swedes would say *Lindkvist* for *Lindquist.*
4. *k* often sounds like *ch,* especially if it has a *j* with it. *Kjell* (a name) is *Chell; kyckling* (chicken) is *chickling.*
5. There is no *w* or *z* in true Swedish words.
6. Certain pronounciation marks change the sound of letters: *ä* is said like the *a* in *late; å* is said like the *o* in *home.*

As you can see from the list below, Swedish and English are related languages.

mother—*moder* or *mor*
father—*fader* or *far*
grandfather—father's father is *farfar;* mother's father
    is *morfar*
sister—*syster*
brother—*broder* or *bror*
book—*bok*
door—*dörr*
princess—*prinsessa*
pumpkin—*pumpa*
ring—*ring*
soldier—*soldat*
student—*student*
Sweden—*Sverige*
Swedish—*Svensk*
uncle—father's brother is *farbror;* mother's brother is
    morbror
table—*bord*
thanks—*tack*
beefsteak—*biffstek*
egg—*ägg*
lamb—*lamm*
tomato—*tomater*
apple—*apple*
fruit—*frukt*

Glossary

doppa i grytan—to dip bread in the water that is used to boil the Christmas ham

du—the word for *you* that is used when speaking to family members or close friends

fågelbo—"bird's nest"; a dish made of a raw egg in a nest of chopped raw meat or fish

filbunke or filmjölk—a food like yogurt that some Swedes eat for breakfast

folkhogskolorna—folk high schools; attended by adults who for some reason did not receive a general education

getost—cheese made from goat's milk

grundskola—a Swedish primary school that is like elementary and junior high school in North America

gymnasium—a Swedish upper school that is like senior high school in North America

hemslöjd—handcrafted sale items that the Swedes make in their homes

julklappar—the funny gifts people in Sweden once gave to each other at Christmastime

klappa—a rap on the door

klocka män—a special doctor who was supposed to be able to cure sicknesses caused by trolls

knäkkebröd—thin, crisp bread that is as big as a large pizza

köttbullar—small and spicy Swedish meatballs

kringle—a pastrylike cream puff

krumkake—a rolled, crisp wafer baked on a special iron that is sometimes filled with cream

lefse—a thin pancake made of potatoes and flour

lingonberries—cranberrylike fruit that grows in Swedish bogs

loppet—a ski race

lutefisk—codfish that is preserved for winter by being dried and soaked in lye

majstång—the maypole that Swedes dance around on Midsummer night

maran—an imaginary creature—human by day, a wolf at night—who was said to bring bad dreams

middag—the midday meal; usually eaten between 4:00 and 6:00 P.M.

necks, nisses—magic spirits that people used to believe in

ni—the word for *you* that is used when speaking to strangers

nornir—fairy godmothers; they are said to bring gifts to new babies and to protect them throughout life

ombudsman—an official who looks into complaints made by citizens about government actions or decisions

rommegrot—pudding made with cream

runes—an ancient form of writing that was carved on stones or written on sheepskin

sandbakkelse—cookies baked in pleated molds; also called sand tarts

skalds—ancient singers who made up songs about heroic deeds and great events

skogsrå—wood trolls

smörgåsbord—a dinner table loaded with a variety of foods that can be chosen for a meal

snäll—quiet and polite

spöken—spooks or ghosts who haunt the places where they are said to have died

spritz—cookies made by squirting dough through a cookie press

strömming—Baltic herring

Tack for maten—"Thank you for the food"

tomte—a helpful spirit that is like a brownie

troll—a wicked, ugly creature with magical powers

tuppen varpte—"The rooster laid an egg"; an old Swedish custom of giving students a reward hidden in the pages of a book

Var så god—"Be so kind"; the Swedish way of saying, "Help yourself"

Selected Bibliography

Anderson, Ingvar. *A History of Sweden.* Translated by Carolyn Hannay. New York: Frederick A. Praeger, 1968.

Bullfinch, Thomas. *Bullfinch's Mythology.* Garden City, New York: Doubleday, 1958.

Friskey, Margaret. *Welcome to Sweden.* Chicago: Children's Press, 1975.

Kastrup, Allan. *The Swedish Heritage in America.* Saint Paul, Minnesota: Swedish Council of America, 1975.

Lagerlof, Selma. *The Wonderful Adventures of Nils.* New York: Doubleday, Page and Co., 1907.

Lindgren, Astrid. *Pippi Longstocking.* New York: Viking Press, 1950.

Lorenzen, Lilly. *Of Swedish Ways.* Minneapolis: Dillon Press, 1964.

Moberg, Vilhelm. *The Emigrants.* Translated by G. Lannestock. New York: Popular Library, 1951.
_____ *Unto a Good Land.* Translated by G. Lannestock. New York: Popular Library, 1954.
_____ *The Settlers.* Translated by G. Lannestock. New York: Popular Library, 1961.

Rehnberg, Mats. *Swedish Holidays and Annual Festivals.* Translated by Alan Tapsell. Stockholm: Swedish Institute, 1964.

Swedish Institute. *Sweden in Brief.* Stockholm: 1981.

Index

142

About the Author

Kari Olsson, a native Minnesotan, has had a lifelong interest in Sweden. The wonderful stories she heard as a child about life in the old country from her mother—who had come to America from Sweden as a teenager—taught her to love and value her Swedish heritage. In later years she came to know modern Sweden well through contacts with relatives who live there. She has written *Sweden: A Good Life for All* in the hope that younger readers will learn more about the Swedes and their contributions to life in North America.

Ms. Olsson enjoys being involved with young people. For many years she taught them in Minnesota's elementary schools, and she has recently begun to write for them. She is the author of two other books, one of them for children.